The Marshall Field's
COOKBOOK

CLASSIC RECIPES and FRESH TAKES from the
FIELD'S CULINARY COUNCIL

TEXT BY
Steve Siegelman

PHOTOGRAPHY BY
Maren Caruso

BOOK
KITCHEN
San Francisco

FIELD'S | MARKETPLACE

CONTENTS

I love good food and discovering great places to eat. And even more than that, I love the traditions that surround food. Over the last century Marshall Field's has created countless culinary traditions, from the perfect popover and classic potpies to Frango cheesecake. With the founding of the Field's Culinary Council and Culinary Studio, we are keeping those traditions alive—and constantly creating new ones, like this cookbook.

I am excited that we are presenting this book to share the history, memories, and flavors of the Walnut Room and the many fine Marshall Field's restaurants, along with cherished family recipes from our talented Culinary Council chefs.

Annual traditions are everywhere at Field's, from the Great Tree in the Walnut Room to the excitement of Culinary Week. And each year it gives me tremendous pleasure to watch new generations being exposed to those traditions and to the timeless pleasures of sharing a special meal.

I know you will enjoy this book as much as I do and have fun looking back at the history, recalling fond food memories, and creating some special meals of your own.

Eat well,
Frank Guzzetta
President and CEO, Marshall Field's

A great department store is a palace of dreams. Its gleaming windows lure us inside to gape at the soaring expanses and wander amid case after case, rack after rack, and room after room of brightly lit treasures. If you've stepped into a world-class department store any time since, well, the mid-1800s, you know that the best of the lot are equal parts museum, theater, social club, and amusement park. But what you might not know is that much of what we think of as the hallmarks of these grand emporiums came from one groundbreaking store and the self-made man who created it.

Marshall Field, Merchant of Dry Goods and Dreams

Marshall Field was, in many ways, an unlikely innovator. He was a shy, serious farm boy from rural Massachusetts, a lad of few words who left school at sixteen to work in a dry goods store a few miles from home in the town of Pittsfield. Small-framed and steely-eyed, he was anything but gregarious. While his colleagues were off carousing at oyster roasts and taffy pulls, he'd spend his evenings reading and endlessly memorizing columns of prices, profits, and figures. But though he may not

"Silent Marsh" at age 24, 1858

have fit the mold of the glad-handing salesman, right from the start Marshall Field showed a keen instinct for the psychology of retail.

To get inside the minds of his customers, young Marshall would pore over *Godey's Lady's Book*, a leading women's monthly of the nineteenth century, studying fashions and tastes. In a little notebook, he recorded the names and preferences of his female customers, and instead of sweet-talking them in the fawning manner of clerks of the day, he would gain their trust by listening attentively and anticipating their needs.

Whether he knew it or not, "Silent Marsh," as his colleagues called him, was quietly inventing a revolutionary, customer-focused approach to retail—an approach that would eventually become his defining motto. Years later, at the peak of his success, while walking through the vast department store that bore his name, Marshall Field overheard a clerk arguing heatedly with a customer. "What are you doing here?" Field asked. "I'm settling a complaint," the clerk replied. "No you're not," said Field. "Give the lady what she wants!" And those famous words remained his credo for the rest of his life.

Go West, Young Marsh

By 1856, after nearly five years as a dry goods clerk, twenty-one-year-old Marshall wanted more. He yearned to move beyond the confines of small-town New England and strike out on his own. Day after day, he would hear stories from customers and traveling salesmen about fortunes being made by enterprising businessmen in the boomtown of the Midwest, Chicago. Field knew he could be one of them. So, with nothing but pocket money and a letter of reference, he moved to Chicago to see for himself. No one—not even Field—could have imagined the kind of success that awaited him.

He found work at the city's big dry goods wholesaling company and quickly rose to become a partner in the business. Within nine years, he and his associate, Levi Leiter, had purchased the Lake Street store of the legendary dry goods magnate, Potter Palmer (who would later open the famed Palmer House Hotel), and in its first year, Field, Leiter, and Company would post sales of eight million dollars.

"What are you doing here?" Field asked. "I'm settling a complaint," the clerk replied. "No you're not," said Field. "Give the lady what she wants!"

What was the secret of their success? Smart buying and attractive prices were part of the equation. But Field knew that the real keys to attracting fickle shoppers were quality merchandise, attractive displays, and, above all, psychological finesse. His approach meant not only treating customers—who were mostly women—with courtesy, respect, and honesty, but also staying a step ahead of their whims and constantly surprising them with new goods and delightful services.

Merchandise was imported from New York and Paris. The store introduced a notions department, stocked with all the supplies a woman could need to make clothing on that new domestic miracle, the sewing machine. Female clerks—a rarity at the time—were hired to help women feel more comfortable buying dresses and intimate apparel. Sweepers kept the entrance on a rough-and-tumble stretch of Lake Street spotless throughout the day. And perhaps the store's biggest enticement of all was its "no questions asked" returns policy—a virtually unheard of practice in its day.

State Street, that Great Street

"The Marble Palace" on State Street, 1868

In 1868, Field and Leiter joined forces with Potter Palmer to move to a newer, larger store. Palmer had begun methodically snatching up sections of narrow, grimy State Street, to the bewilderment of many Chicagoans. But soon, as he began razing buildings and widening the street, his designs became clear. Before long, what would be known as the Marble Palace, an ornate, six-story marvel, rose gleaming white from the mud and rubble. Field and Leiter moved in, and the Marshall Field's style of definitive elegance and dazzling quality began in earnest.

The *Chicago Tribune* called the opening of Field, Leiter, and Company "the grandest affair of its kind which ever transpired in Chicago, the city of grand affairs." Gentlemen were greeted with cigars and ladies, with roses. Inside, they stared in wonder at the frescoed walls and polished walnut counters. Gas lamps dramatically illuminated the dazzling merchandise—Persian cashmere shawls priced at $1,200 (about $24,000 in today's money), sealskin cloaks, embroidered silks, and the finest velvets and furs in the world.

Field and Leiter knew that splashy wares like these would help them create a unique shopping experience that no other store could match. So, in a bold move, they became the first American department store to set up a European buying office, run by Field's brother, Joseph, in Manchester, England. The strategy paid off. Customers of every social background, from Chicago's high society and post–Civil War nouveau riche to its working-class shoppers flooded the Marble Palace to try on the "special Parisian frocks" and Scottish tweeds—or simply to wander from room to room, marveling at the exquisite luxury of it all.

Marshall Field, Levi Leiter, and Potter Palmer had created the great American department store—a one-of-a-kind shopping destination with a reputation for quality and profusion. Meanwhile, a new class of women shoppers was shedding their hoopskirts and crinoline and stepping out into the world. They were hungry for service, eager to be heard, and ready to spend. And for them, every trip to the Marble Palace was a little voyage of discovery. They'd be sure to find just what they wanted—even if they didn't yet know they wanted it.

For a Victorian lady, the thought of moving about unescorted in public was unheard of. Restaurants and cafes would not seat an unaccompanied woman. There were no tearooms or private clubs for ladies, no hairdressers or beauty shops. But within the walls of Field and Leiter, a woman was welcome on her own terms. She was received as a lady, whatever her social status. She could browse for hours, socialize with friends, buy on credit so she'd never have to carry cash, and have her purchases delivered directly to her home. The Marble Palace was her Eden—a haven, designed in every detail for convenience and pleasure. But within three years, it would be gone forever.

FIELD'S FIRSTS

Much of what is now standard practice in department stores everywhere was pioneered at Marshall Field's. Here's a partial listing:

The bridal registry

The women's restroom

Fixed, guaranteed pricing

Satisfaction guaranteed returns policy

Fully realized scenes in window displays

Widespread use of electric lighting

The bargain basement

A European buying office

Food service

Flames and Fortune

On Sunday, October 8, 1871, the Great Chicago Fire ravaged most of the city, and Field and Leiter was destroyed. The intense heat reduced its marble to smoldering dust, leaving nothing more than a heap of twisted steel. But in the hours before the blaze had reached State Street, much of the inventory had been saved.

The Great Chicago Fire reduced the Marble Palace to smoldering dust and twisted steel.

Field was adamant that the company must stay in business and immediately leased an old Chicago City Railway horse barn farther up State Street to house a temporary store. Loyal employees volunteered to help. Oat bins, harnesses, and hay bales were cleared away. Stalls were whitewashed and pine counters hastily installed. The inventory was restocked, new merchandise was rushed in from New York, and within two weeks, Field and Leiter were back in business.

Their swift recovery was a public relations coup, and they were praised as models of industrious optimism in the face of disaster. Eager to get back to business as usual, Chicagoans thronged the old horse barn by the thousands.

Later that year, the partners built a store at Madison and Market Streets, and in 1873, they moved back to State Street. But that store, too, was destroyed by fire in 1877. In 1879, Field and Leiter was reborn for a third time at its current location at State and Washington Streets. In 1881, Field bought out his partner, and renamed the store Marshall Field and Company. He would reign as Chicago's "merchant prince" until his death in 1906.

Marshall Field's commitment to quality, selection, and honesty was a model for many of the finest stores in the world. But he left an even greater legacy. It was, in his day, what many regarded as a topsy-turvy way of looking at commerce. Instead of wondering, "What can I sell?" he asked, "What do you want?" And with that simple question, Marshall Field redefined the business of retail forever.

A Visual Feast

Marshall Field's flagship State Street store ranks among the top tourist destinations in Chicago, welcoming more than nine million visitors a year. The second largest department store in the United States, it covers a full city block, with a staggering eight hundred thousand square feet of retail space on fourteen floors. The building, in its current form, was completed in 1907, a year after Marshall Field's death, under the direction of company president, John Shedd.

Wanting to bring the store's design together with an overarching symbol of splendor and elegance, Shedd commissioned Louis Comfort Tiffany to create a mosaic to adorn the central light well. Tiffany designed a vast dome, spanning six thousand square feet at the sixth-floor level of the store, and decorated it with 1.6 million pieces of his signature iridescent Favrile glass. It would be flooded with sunlight during the day and illuminated by a new system of dazzling electric lights by night. Still as breathtaking as ever, the Tiffany dome remains the largest unbroken example of Tiffany Favrile in the world.

MEET ME UNDER THE CLOCK—The great clocks of Marshall Field's have kept Chicago on time for more than a century. The clock at State and Washington was installed in 1897, and its twin, on the corner of State and Randolph, a decade later. And ever since, "Meet me under the clock" has been a Chicago tradition. Elegantly cantilevered from the corners of the building like ornaments on a Gothic cathedral, they appear to float over the sidewalk. But don't be fooled. Each cast bronze clock weighs more than seven tons—as much as a full-grown Tyrannosaurus rex! Light bulbs illuminate the clocks' faces from within and also help to keep the clockworks warm and dry.

THE ART OF WINDOW SHOPPING—In 1895, most stores used their street-facing windows simply to display samples of their merchandise. But Field's great display genius, Arthur Valair Fraser, changed all that. He began creating set pieces along thematic lines, often spending months building scale models and doing research. To showcase a silver service, he recreated the setting of a millionaire's mansion, complete with paneled walls and thousands of dollars worth of furniture. His creations attracted throngs of curious onlookers, and the notion of "window shopping" was born. Fraser reigned supreme at Field's well into the 1920s. And the State Street windows have been drawing crowds ever since.

FOOD AT FIELD'S

The Walnut Room—It All Started with a Humble Pie

By 1890, Marshall Field's had established itself as a place where ladies were welcome to congregate. But there was just one thing missing: food. That's when Mrs. Hering came along. An enterprising clerk in the State Street millinery department, she had been trained in Field's "give the lady what she wants" tradition of customer service. When she overheard two customers grumbling that they had nowhere to eat, she thought nothing of offering them the homemade chicken potpie she had brought for lunch. She set up a table, served up her pie, and, without knowing it, started a restaurant—and a revolution.

The ladies spread the word about the tasty meal they'd enjoyed, and soon Mrs. Hering was selling her pies at a counter in the millinery department. A young manager named Harry Selfridge (who would go on to found Selfridges Department Store in London, modeling it after Field's) was quick to recognize the potential of serving food to hungry guests, and thus keeping them in the store for more shopping. So he persuaded Field to try out the idea by opening a small tearoom in the building.

On April 15, 1890, fifteen tables were set up on the third floor. There were eight waitresses and four cooks. Each plate was adorned with a red rose. That day, fifty-six women turned up to lunch on corned beef hash, chicken salad, orange punch in an orange shell, and, of course, Mrs. Hering's chicken potpies.

Selfridge's hunch paid off. The South Tearoom, the world's first restaurant in a department store, was a runaway hit. It was quickly expanded and within a year was serving fifteen hundred guests a day. In the tradition of Mrs. Hering, many of the cooks in those early days prepared their specialties—from codfish cakes to Boston baked beans—in their own home kitchens and brought them in each morning.

When it moved to its current location on the seventh floor, the tearoom expanded to seventeen thousand square feet. It took its new name from the Circassian walnut that was imported from Russia to panel the walls. Today, during peak season, as many as five thousand guests a day line up along the red ropes outside the Walnut Room, and more than a century later, Mrs. Hering's potpies are still the top-selling item on the menu.

Tea for Two—or Two Thousand

Field's elaborate tea parties became legendary starting in the 1920s. Back then guests were greeted with finger bowls filled with warm water; rose petals and mint leaves were scattered on their plates; and delicate sandwiches and teacakes were served from doily-lined baskets. To finish, there was lemon ice or homemade pineapple sherbet, served in tall stemware.

The waitresses—known until the 1930s as "maids"—wore white aprons over long-sleeved, high-necked black dresses with bishop's collars and stiff cuffs. Field's had a strict "no bob" policy, so waitresses tied back their long hair with white bows.

Tea service is still very much a part of the Walnut Room, where the phrase "high tea" takes on a whole new meaning. Seven stories above Chicago, guests gaze out on a splendid panorama of the city. And as afternoon light streams through the stately windows, they enjoy the civilized pleasures of finger sandwiches, scones, cookies, cakes, and tarts, all washed down with a sturdy cup of tea.

LEFT: "I always have tea or a little something at Field's" says Estelle Jones Langston, who grew up in Chicago. ABOVE: Elizabeth Wallace and Agnes Hagen serve tea in the 1940s.

The Narcissus Room

The Men's Grill

From Tea Service to Full-Service

The Walnut Room soon became one of several restaurants on the State Street store's seventh floor.

The Narcissus Room, named for its central fountain featuring a statue of Narcissus, opened in 1914. With its Roman mosaic floor, classical columns, and sweeping views of Lake Michigan, the restaurant was a popular teatime destination for most of the twentieth century. Today, it is used as a venue for parties and special events.

Other restaurants and tearooms followed, including the Mission Grill Room, the Crystal Tea Room, the Wedgwood Room, and the quick-service Colonial Tea Room. There were also oak-paneled dining rooms, some featuring open grills where steaks and chops were broiled in full view of the customers, long before "exhibition cooking" became trendy.

In time, the State Street building had so many restaurants that an on-premise butcher shop, bakery, and candy shop were added to support them. By the mid-1920s, Marshall Field's tearooms and grills occupied one hundred thousand square feet— more space than an entire city block—and served up to eight thousand people a day.

Twentieth-Century Tastemaker

Throughout the twentieth century, Marshall Field and Company established a reputation for great food. During the 1930s, the Men's Grill did a brisk business on the sixth floor of the Store for Men. Offering "all the comfort of a club without the dues," it served upwards of a thousand men—and only men—a day until 1946.

In 1948, its successor, the English Grill (sometimes known as the North Grill Room) was opened on the seventh floor of the State Street store. Women were now admitted, but for many years, the grill maintained a "men only" section.

The Cloud Room

That same year, Field's opened a new restaurant with a futuristic design at the recently built South Cicero Avenue terminal of Midway Airport. At the grand opening of the swank Cloud Room, guests feasted on delicacies flown in from around the world— potatoes from Bermuda, lobster from Africa, pineapple from Hawaii, and strawberries from California. The Cloud Room became one of the hottest tickets in Chicago fine dining. Seated beneath an Alexander Calder mobile, diners could watch the planes take off and land on the tarmac below and rub elbows with the jet-set celebrities of the day.

Dayton's and Hudson's Bring their Beloved Traditions to the Table

Dining traditions have never stopped evolving at Field's. In 1990, Marshall Field's joined forces with Minneapolis-based Dayton's and Detroit-based Hudson's, bringing together their own flagship restaurants and menu specialties. In 2001, the three were united under the Marshall Field's banner. From Dayton's came regional dishes, such as Boundary Waters Wild Rice Soup and perennial favorites like Mandarin Chicken Salad and Popovers. Hudson's brought its famed Canadian Cheese Soup and the phenomenally popular Maurice Salad to Field's menus.

Dayton's Sky Room, Minneapolis, 1961

Hudson's Georgian Room, Detroit, 1920s

In the Twin Cities, 1947 saw the opening of three favorite dining destinations. The clubby Oak Grill, designed by architect Bob Hansen, is a perennial downtown Minneapolis favorite. Its ornate fireplace from Salisbury, England, was more than three hundred years old when it was transported in sections to the restaurant. Next door, the recently remodeled Sky Room represents the other end of the spectrum with its sleek, ultramodern design, sweeping views of the surrounding skyscrapers, and state-of-the-plate lunch options. And across the river, in Saint Paul, the elegant River Room has been a local dining institution for decades.

The original downtown Detroit Hudson's location housed many culinary retreats for hungry guests. The thirteenth floor was home to several restaurants, including the Pine Room, the Georgian Room, and the Early American Room, which later evolved into the Riverview Room. The store also offered a tearoom, snack bar, bakery, and fine wine shop, among other specialty food and dining venues. Though Detroit's downtown historical gem closed in 1983, many of its culinary traditions have been passed on to its other Hudson's locations. Now under the Marshall Field's name, Hudson's favorites continue to delight beyond Michigan.

Among the company's brightest stars in recent years are its twelve Lakeshore Grills in the Minneapolis, Chicago, and Detroit areas, where guests enjoy spit-cooked rotisserie specialties along with all the Field's, Dayton's, and Hudson's classics.

Today, Field's menus—and the recipes in this book—offer the best of these three world-class department stores: great American and international food, famous for pleasing crowds and perfect for sharing with family and friends.

A New Culinary Millennium

In its third century, Marshall Field's has reached a new level of fresh, contemporary excitement with the 2003 debut of the Field's Culinary Council, an advisory committee made up of a dozen of the nation's leading culinary stars (see page 117). These chefs consult on menus and culinary products, create recipes for Field's restaurants, and make year-round appearances at the stores—teaching classes, signing books, and greeting and feeding their fans.

In 2004, Field's gave the Council a home of its own—a state-of-the-art Culinary Studio, a kitchen classroom where Council chefs and scores of other food experts present a regular schedule of classes, demonstrations, and special food events. Housed on the seventh floor of the State Street store, the forty-two thousand square-foot studio features bistro seating for eighty guests.

Memories, Favorites and Fresh Ideas

For more than 150 years, Marshall Field and Company has helped define and shape American tastes. And when it comes to food, no other department store can look back on such a bountiful history of beloved culinary traditions. In September 2006, Marshall Field's will become part of the Macy's family of stores. Its name will be gone, but those cherished traditions will remain.

After all, by any name, the great culinary signatures of Marshall Field's—the Walnut Room, the restaurants and tearooms past and present, the Field's food products and wines, the Culinary Council and Studio, the millions of chicken potpies, and the billions of Frango chocolates—all add up to a single thing: an abiding passion for food.

And that passion is what this book is really all about. In these pages, you'll find recipes for your favorite Field's classics—from salads, sandwiches, appetizers, and entrées, to Frango desserts and delightful holiday treats. You'll also find contemporary twists on those classics along with beloved family recipes from the chefs of the Field's Culinary Council.

Those chefs and the twenty-five thousand men and women of the Marshall Field's team proudly offer you this book as a keepsake. If it sparks a few memories and makes you head for the stove, they'll be happy. Because as long as your kitchen is filled with the aromas of potpies and popovers, the spirit of food and friendship at Field's will always have a home.

THE CLASSICS

Marshall Field's Favorites to Enjoy at Home

BOUNDARY WATERS WILD RICE SOUP

Serves 6

Wild rice is one of the great culinary icons of Minnesota, and this hearty soup, created at the Oak Grill in the Minneapolis store, pays tribute to that tradition. It's named for the region of lakes that hugs the Canadian border in the northeast corner of the state, where wild rice grows.

Melt the butter in a large saucepan over medium heat. Add the onion and sauté for 5 minutes, until translucent. Add the leek, mushrooms, and carrots and cook, stirring occasionally, for 5 minutes, until softened.

Add the flour and cook, stirring constantly, for 1 minute. Whisk in the chicken broth. Bring to a boil, then decrease the heat and simmer for 20 minutes. Add the rice, chicken meat, cream, sherry, salt, pepper, parsley, and thyme and cook for 5 minutes, until warmed through. Taste and adjust the seasoning as necessary. Garnish with the almonds and serve hot. (To store, allow the soup to cool to room temperature, cover, and refrigerate for up to 3 days.)

6 tablespoons unsalted butter

1 cup diced yellow onion

1 small leek, halved lengthwise, rinsed well, and thinly sliced

$1^1/_2$ cups sliced button mushrooms

$^3/_4$ cup diced carrots

$^1/_2$ cup all-purpose flour

6 cups chicken broth

$1^1/_2$ cups cooked wild rice

$^1/_2$ roasted chicken, meat chopped (1 to $1^1/_2$ cups)

1 cup heavy cream

5 tablespoons dry sherry

2 teaspoons salt

$1^1/_2$ teaspoons freshly ground black pepper

2 tablespoons chopped fresh flat-leaf parsley

1 teaspoon chopped fresh thyme leaves

2 tablespoons slivered almonds, toasted, for garnish (see page 32)

SPICED BUTTERNUT SQUASH SOUP

with Ham-Apple-Pecan Relish

Serves 6 to 8

Think of your favorite fall flavor combinations—squash and apples, pecans and maple syrup, ginger and cinnamon. This silky, golden soup topped with a fresh, crunchy relish has them all. To get the consistency just right, start with just enough broth to cook the squash. After you purée it, add more liquid as needed—it's easier to thin a soup than to thicken it.

TO PREPARE THE RELISH, combine all the ingredients in a bowl and toss to blend thoroughly. Taste and adjust the seasoning as necessary. Use immediately or cover and refrigerate for up to 24 hours. (The relish is best just after it is made.)

Heat the oil in a large pot over medium heat. Add the onion and cook for 5 minutes, until translucent. Add the garlic and cook, stirring, for 2 minutes. Add the carrots and squash and cook for 5 minutes, until just beginning to soften. Pour the broth over the vegetables to cover. Add a little more broth if the vegetables are not completely covered. Bring to a boil, then decrease the heat to a simmer. Cover and cook for about 30 minutes, until the squash is very tender.

Add the ginger, cinnamon, and roasted garlic. Working in batches as necessary, transfer the soup to a blender and purée until smooth (or use an immersion blender). If the soup is too thick and has the consistency of applesauce, add more broth to thin it to the desired consistency. Stir in the cream, maple syrup, salt, and pepper and taste for seasoning. Serve hot, topped with a generous portion of the relish.

HAM-APPLE-PECAN RELISH

1 cup chopped pecans, toasted (see page 32)

1/3 cup finely minced fresh chives

1 Braeburn or other tart crisp apple, diced

1 cup finely diced ham

2 teaspoons seeded and finely minced jalapeño chile

Juice of 1/2 lime

1 tablespoon pure maple syrup

1/2 teaspoon salt

1/2 teaspoon freshly ground black pepper

2 tablespoons extra virgin olive oil

1 cup chopped yellow onion

1 tablespoon minced garlic

2 carrots, chopped

1 (2-pound) butternut squash, peeled, seeded, and diced

4 cups chicken broth, plus more if needed

1 tablespoon minced fresh ginger

1/4 teaspoon ground cinnamon

1 tablespoon chopped roasted garlic cloves (see page 61)

1/4 cup heavy cream

2 tablespoons pure maple syrup

1 teaspoon salt

1 teaspoon freshly ground black pepper

CANADIAN CHEESE SOUP

Serves 6

This rich, creamy soup has been a fixture on the menu in Detroit—first at Hudson's, then at Marshall Field's—for more than two decades. To get the best flavor and texture, use a high-quality aged cheddar. For a tasty "grilled cheese" effect, you can garnish each bowlful with buttery pan-toasted French bread croutons.

Place a large saucepan over medium heat and add the butter. When the butter is melted, add the onion, celery, and carrot and cook, stirring, for about 10 minutes, until the vegetables are soft. Sprinkle the flour and paprika over the vegetables and stir for 1 minute. Whisk in the milk and broth and bring to a simmer. Simmer, whisking occasionally, for 10 minutes, until thickened. Decrease the heat to low and whisk in the cheese, salt, and pepper. Stir until the cheese is completely melted and incorporated. Taste and adjust the seasoning as necessary. Serve hot.

4 tablespoons unsalted butter

1 tablespoon finely chopped onion

$1/2$ cup finely diced celery

$1/2$ cup finely diced carrot

$1/2$ cup all-purpose flour

$1/2$ teaspoon paprika

3 cups whole milk

3 cups chicken broth

2 pounds aged sharp cheddar cheese, shredded

$1/2$ teaspoon salt

1 teaspoon freshly ground black pepper

LOBSTER BISQUE

Serves 6

There's no question about it: this is a fancy, special-occasion splurge. That explains why it's such a huge seller during the holidays at the Walnut Room. It's really best when you start with live lobsters. If you go that route, place the lobsters in boiling salted water for 3 minutes, then drain, cool, and continue with the recipe as directed.

Use a heavy knife or poultry shears to separate the tails and claws from the bodies of the lobsters. Place a large, heavy-bottomed stockpot over medium-high heat and add the butter. When the butter is melted, sauté the lobster tails, claws, and bodies, stirring frequently, for 5 minutes. Remove the pot from the heat and take out the lobster with tongs, leaving the butter in the pot. When cool enough to handle, remove the meat from the tails and claws, chop into bite-size pieces, cover, and refrigerate. Reserve the shells, bodies, and legs.

Return the pot to medium heat and add the carrots, celery, tomatoes, garlic, shallots, and tarragon. Sauté for 10 minutes, until the vegetables are soft. Stir in the tomato paste and cook for 1 minute. Pour in the Cognac and carefully ignite with a long match. When the Cognac has evaporated, sprinkle the flour over the vegetables and stir for 1 minute. Whisk in the wine and bring to a simmer. Add the broth and the reserved lobster shells, bodies, and legs. Add the thyme and bay leaf and season with salt, pepper, and cayenne to taste. Decrease the heat to medium-low and simmer gently for 45 minutes.

Remove all the shells from the soup and discard. Working in batches as necessary, transfer the soup to a blender and purée until smooth (or use an immersion blender). Pass through a fine-mesh strainer into a large saucepan and return to medium-low heat. Simmer for a few minutes, until thickened. Stir in the cream. Taste and adjust the seasoning as necessary. Stir in the reserved lobster meat.

Divide among bowls and garnish with the chives. Finish with a splash of sherry and serve at once.

3 (1 to 1 1/4-pound) cooked lobsters

6 tablespoons unsalted butter

2 carrots, chopped

2 celery stalks, chopped

2 tomatoes, chopped

1 1/2 tablespoons chopped garlic

1 cup chopped shallots

2 tablespoons fresh tarragon leaves

3 tablespoons tomato paste

1/4 cup Cognac

6 tablespoons all-purpose flour

2 cups dry white wine

10 cups fish broth, or 4 cups chicken broth and 6 cups water

1/2 teaspoon dried thyme

1 bay leaf

Salt and freshly ground black pepper

Ground cayenne pepper

2 cups heavy whipping cream

1 tablespoon chopped fresh chives or parsley, for garnish

Splash of dry sherry (optional)

MANDARIN CHICKEN SALAD

Serves 4 | *This colorful Asian-style salad is a showstopper—especially when you garnish it with crispy wonton strips. To save time you can substitute store-bought crispy chow mein noodles or fried wontons. Field's bottled Toasted Sesame Dressing is one of the company's most popular retail food items. And now you have the secret recipe.*

TO PREPARE THE CHICKEN AND MARINADE, combine the soy sauce, orange juice, green onions, and garlic in a shallow bowl. Add the chicken, toss well to coat, and cover with plastic wrap. Refrigerate for at least 30 minutes or up to overnight. Preheat the broiler and position the rack 4 to 5 inches from the heating element. Place the chicken in a broiler pan and cook, turning once, for about 20 minutes, until lightly browned. Remove from the oven, allow to cool to room temperature, then cover and refrigerate until chilled. Slice the chicken into strips.

TO PREPARE THE WONTONS, pour the oil in a large saucepan to a depth of several inches. Place over medium-high heat. When the oil is hot, add the wonton strips a few at a time and fry for about 1 minute, until crisp and golden. With a slotted spoon, transfer to paper towels to drain. The fried wontons can be stored in an airtight container for up to 24 hours.

TO PREPARE THE DRESSING, combine the sugar, vinegar, onion juice, soy sauce, and mustard in a blender or food processor and blend well. With the motor running, add the oil in a slow, steady stream to make an emulsion. Stir in the sesame seeds and salt to taste.

Place a large skillet over medium-high heat. Add the bacon and cook, turning, until crisped. Transfer to paper towels to drain and cool. Chop the bacon.

Bring a saucepan full of water to a boil over high heat. Fill a bowl with ice water. Submerge the snow peas into the boiling water for no more than 1 minute, until they turn brilliant green. Immediately drain and place into the ice water. Drain again, then cut in half on the diagonal.

continued

CHICKEN AND MARINADE

$1/2$ cup soy sauce

$1/4$ cup freshly squeezed orange juice

2 green onions, thinly sliced

1 clove garlic, minced

1 pound boneless skinless chicken breasts

FRIED WONTONS

Vegetable oil, for frying

6 wonton skins, cut into $1/4$-inch strips

TOASTED SESAME DRESSING

$1/3$ cup sugar

3 tablespoons apple cider vinegar

$2 1/4$ teaspoons onion juice (see page 33)

1 teaspoon soy sauce

$1/2$ teaspoon dry mustard

$1/2$ cup vegetable oil

1 tablespoon sesame seeds, toasted (see note)

Salt

TO ASSEMBLE THE SALAD, combine the chicken, bacon, snow peas, bell peppers, water chestnuts, oranges, green onions, and lettuces in a large bowl. Add the dressing and toss lightly. Divide among 4 chilled plates, top each salad with the wontons, garnish with the almonds and sesame seeds, and serve.

TOASTING SESAME SEEDS: Toast sesame seeds in a dry skillet over medium heat, shaking the pan occasionally, for 3 to 5 minutes, until the seeds are golden brown and fragrant.

TOASTING NUTS: To toast nuts, such as almonds, hazelnuts, pecans, pistachios, or walnuts, preheat the oven to 350°F, line a baking sheet with parchment paper, and spread the nuts on the baking sheet in a single layer. Bake for 7 to 10 minutes, until the nuts are lightly browned and fragrant, shaking the pan once or twice.

SALAD

5 strips bacon

1 cup snow peas

$1/4$ cup diced red bell peppers

1 (8-ounce) can sliced water chestnuts, drained

1 (11-ounce) can mandarin oranges, drained

2 green onions, thinly sliced

$1/2$ head romaine lettuce, sliced (about $2 1/2$ cups)

$1/2$ head iceberg lettuce, sliced (about $2 1/2$ cups)

$1/4$ cup sliced almonds, toasted, for garnish (see note)

2 tablespoons black sesame seeds or toasted sesame seeds, for garnish (see note)

MAURICE SALAD

Serves 4 to 6

Who was Maurice? Some say he was chef at Hudson's in Detroit (which later became Marshall Field's), where this salad made its debut, though no one knows for sure. While Maurice's identity may have faded into obscurity, his chef's salad with a lemony mayo dressing remains the number-one seller in all of Field's Michigan restaurants. Look for small bottles of onion juice in the spice section of many supermarkets. If it's not available, grate a piece of onion and squeeze the pulp through cheesecloth or a fine-mesh strainer.

TO PREPARE THE DRESSING, combine the vinegar, lemon juice, onion juice, sugar, Dijon, and dry mustard in a bowl and whisk well to dissolve the sugar. Whisk in the mayonnaise, parsley, and egg and season with salt and pepper to taste.

In a large bowl, combine the ham, turkey, cheese, and pickles and toss lightly. Pour the dressing over the salad and gently fold together. Arrange a bed of the lettuce on each plate. Top with the meat and cheese mixture and garnish each serving with 2 olives. Serve at once.

MAURICE DRESSING

2 teaspoons distilled white vinegar

1$1/2$ teaspoons freshly squeezed lemon juice

1$1/2$ teaspoons onion juice

1$1/2$ teaspoons sugar

1$1/2$ teaspoons Dijon mustard

$1/4$ teaspoon dry mustard

1 cup mayonnaise

2 tablespoons chopped fresh parsley

1 hard-boiled egg, diced

Salt and freshly ground black pepper

1 pound ham, julienned

1 pound cooked turkey breast, julienned

1 pound Swiss cheese, julienned

$1/2$ cup slivered sweet gherkin pickles

1 head iceberg lettuce, shredded

8 to 12 pimiento-stuffed green olives, for garnish

STRAWBERRY CHICKEN SALAD

Serves 4 | *Any kind of cooked chicken or turkey tastes good in this salad, but grilled boneless chicken breasts are the Walnut Room way to go. Season them with simply with salt, pepper, and olive oil and cook them on a grill, in the broiler, or using a grill pan. The bright, fresh tomato vinaigrette perfectly ties together all the sweet and savory flavors.*

TO PREPARE THE VINAIGRETTE, combine the tomatoes, garlic, shallots, vinegar, and mustard in a blender and purée until smooth. With the motor running, add the oil in a slow, steady stream to make an emulsion. Add the salt and pepper and taste for seasoning. The vinaigrette can be covered and refrigerated for up to 5 days.

Place the spinach in a large bowl and toss with $1/2$ cup of the vinaigrette. Season to taste with salt and pepper. Divide the spinach among 4 chilled plates. Arrange the onion, chicken, and strawberries on top of the spinach. Sprinkle with the feta and walnuts. Drizzle a little of the vinaigrette over the chicken and serve at once.

TOMATO-BALSAMIC VINAIGRETTE
Makes about $2^1/_2$ cups

2 large Roma tomatoes, diced

1 tablespoon minced garlic

$1/_4$ cup minced shallots

$1/_2$ cup balsamic vinegar

2 teaspoons Dijon mustard

1 cup olive oil

$1/_2$ teaspoon salt

$1/_2$ teaspoon freshly ground black pepper

6 ounces baby spinach

Salt and freshly ground black pepper

$1/_2$ small red onion, julienned

4 grilled chicken breasts, cooled and thinly sliced (or meat from 1 roasted chicken pulled into bite-size pieces)

1 cup thinly sliced fresh strawberries

$1/_2$ cup crumbled feta cheese

$1/_2$ cup candied walnuts (see page 195)

SEARED SCALLOP SALAD with Caramelized Pineapple Vinaigrette

Serves 4

This splashy first course salad gets its exotic flavor from a clever trick: caramelizing pineapple. The scallops are caramelized too, bringing out their sweetness and giving them a delicate crust. When caramelizing the scallops, avoid the temptation to use a nonstick pan and go for a heavy stainless steel or cast-iron skillet. Heat the oil until it's very hot and don't touch the scallops once you put them in the pan, except to turn them once. You can also make this recipe with shrimp or chunks of boneless, skinless chicken breasts. Look for togarashi (a spicy Japanese red chile powder) and sambal oelek (a Southeast Asian chile paste) at Asian markets and some grocery stores.

TO PREPARE THE VINAIGRETTE, place a large saucepan over medium-high heat and add the butter. When the butter is melted, add the sugar and pineapple and cook, stirring often, for about 15 minutes, until the pineapple is caramelized and golden brown. Watch closely so it doesn't burn. Remove from the heat and allow to cool slightly.

Combine the pineapple and any juices from the pan, vinegar, lime juice, ginger, togarashi powder, salt, pepper, and sesame oil in a blender. Blend on high speed until smooth. With the motor running, add the vegetable oil in a slow, steady stream to make an emulsion. Taste and adjust the seasoning as necessary and stir in the sesame seeds. Use immediately or cover and refrigerate for up to 2 days.

In a bowl, combine the scallops, sesame oil, 3 of the green onions, garlic, ginger, chile paste, salt, and pepper and toss gently to coat. Cover and refrigerate for at least 1 hour or up to 2 days.

CARAMELIZED PINEAPPLE
VINAIGRETTE

1 tablespoon unsalted butter

1 tablespoon sugar

1$1/2$ cups diced pineapple

2 tablespoons rice wine vinegar

1$1/2$ teaspoons freshly squeezed lime juice

$1/2$ teaspoon minced fresh ginger

$1/8$ teaspoon togarashi powder or ground cayenne pepper

$1/8$ teaspoon salt

$1/8$ teaspoon freshly ground black pepper

$1/2$ teaspoon sesame oil

6 tablespoons vegetable oil

$1/2$ teaspoon black sesame seeds or toasted sesame seeds (see page 32)

1$1/2$ pounds large sea scallops, halved crosswise

1 tablespoon sesame oil

1 bunch plus 3 green onions, thinly sliced

2 teaspoons minced garlic

2 teaspoons minced fresh ginger

2 teaspoons sambal oelek chile paste

$1/2$ teaspoon salt

In a large bowl, combine the cabbage, lettuce, carrots, bell pepper, and remaining green onions and toss lightly. Add $\frac{1}{2}$ cup of the vinaigrette, season to taste with salt and pepper, and toss well. Divide equally among 4 large plates.

Place a large skillet over high heat and add the oil. When the oil shimmers, add the scallops one at a time, being careful not to crowd them. Sear for 1 minute on each side, until browned. Divide the scallops equally on top of the salads. Drizzle the scallops with a little more vinaigrette and top with the potatoes. Serve immediately.

$\frac{1}{2}$ teaspoon freshly ground black pepper

$\frac{1}{2}$ head napa cabbage, julienned (about 2$\frac{1}{2}$ cups)

$\frac{1}{2}$ head romaine lettuce, julienned (about 2$\frac{1}{2}$ cups)

1 cup julienned carrots

1 red bell pepper, julienned

2 tablespoons peanut or grapeseed oil

1 cup homemade or canned shoestring potatoes (see page 45)

WHITE MEAT CHICKEN SALAD

Serves 4 to 6

At the State Street store, the chefs cook hundreds of pounds of chicken every day to use in salads. Years ago, they developed this foolproof oven-poaching technique that produces moist, tender white meat. You can use this method when preparing any of the chicken salads in this book. White Meat Chicken Salad is served in sandwiches and salads at Marketplace, and is also the star of the Walnut Room's famed Peach Basket Salad (see note; pictured at left).

Preheat the oven to 375°F. Lightly coat a large rimmed baking sheet with nonstick spray. Season the chicken liberally on both sides with salt and pepper and arrange in an even layer on the prepared baking sheet. Carefully pour water around the chicken to a depth of about $1/4$ inch. Cover the pan tightly with aluminum foil and poach for 30 minutes, until just cooked through. Remove the foil and allow the chicken to cool to room temperature in the liquid. Transfer the chicken to a cutting board and cut into $1/2$-inch dice.

In a large bowl, combine the chicken, celery, mayonnaise, lemon juice, and Worcestershire sauce and toss well to combine thoroughly. Season to taste with salt and pepper. Serve immediately or cover and refrigerate for up to 3 days.

PEACH BASKET SALAD: Place a large leaf of lettuce on a plate. Place a mound of shoestring potatoes (see page 45) on the lettuce. Top the potatoes with a large scoop of the chicken salad. Sprinkle 1 tablespoon sliced almonds over the chicken. Arrange 3 slices canned peaches next to the chicken salad. Thinly spread $1/2$ slice date-nut bread, $1/2$ slice zucchini bread, and $1/2$ slice pound cake with whipped cream cheese and arrange next to the chicken salad as well. Garnish with 2 fresh strawberries.

$2 1/2$ pounds boneless skinless chicken breasts

Salt and freshly ground black pepper

$1 1/2$ cups chopped celery

$1 1/4$ cups mayonnaise

2 tablespoons freshly squeezed lemon juice

2 teaspoons Worcestershire sauce

FIELD'S SPECIAL

Serves 4 *No one at Marshall Field's can account for the phenomenal popularity of this unusual item—a cross between an open-faced turkey club and a wedge salad. It's been on the menu for more than sixty years, and the Field's kitchen staff has given it all kinds of pet names, including "the Cyclops." When it was retired a few years ago to make room for something more contemporary, people just kept ordering it anyway, so now it's back on the menu to stay. Try it and you'll see why.*

TO PREPARE THE DRESSING, whisk all the ingredients together in a small bowl until well combined. Use immediately or cover and refrigerate for up to 5 days.

Place a large skillet over medium-high heat. Add the bacon and cook, turning, until crisped. Transfer to paper towels to drain.

Spread each slice of bread with butter. Place 1 slice of bread on each of 4 plates.

Reserving 8 large outer leaves of lettuce, core the rest of the head of lettuce and cut into 6 lengthwise slices. Place 1 slice on each piece of bread (reserve the remaining 2 slices for another use). Place 2 slices of cheese diagonally atop each sandwich. Top each with 2 of the reserved whole lettuce leaves.

Arrange 3 slices of turkey over the lettuce, then pour $1/2$ cup of the dressing over each serving of turkey. Add a slice of tomato and top with a slice of egg. Secure the olives to the sandwiches with toothpicks, spearing them into the egg and tomato. Arrange 2 slices of bacon next to each sandwich and serve.

THOUSAND ISLAND SALAD DRESSING

1 cup mayonnaise

1 cup chili sauce

2 teaspoons Dijon mustard

1 teaspoon apple cider vinegar

1 teaspoon sugar

1 hard-boiled egg, chopped

$1/4$ cup chopped dill pickle

2 tablespoons minced onion

$1/4$ teaspoon salt

$1/4$ teaspoon freshly ground black pepper

8 slices bacon

4 large slices deli-style rye bread, bottom crust removed

2 tablespoons unsalted butter, at room temperature

1 head iceberg lettuce

8 (1-ounce) slices Swiss cheese

12 (1-ounce) slices turkey breast

4 tomato slices

4 slices hard-boiled egg

4 pitted black olives

CHOPPED SALAD with White Balsamic Vinaigrette

Serves 4

If you love the flavors of an Italian antipasto platter, this main-dish salad is for you. The recipe makes lots of extra dressing, which, you'll discover, is a good thing—it's great on any kind of green salad or pasta salad. An entire bunch of basil may seem like a lot, but don't hold back—it's a key ingredient in the mix here.

TO PREPARE THE VINAIGRETTE, combine the vinegar, egg, shallots, mustard, salt, and pepper in a blender and process to combine. With the motor running, add the oil in a slow, steady stream to make an emulsion. Adjust the seasoning with salt and pepper as necessary. The vinaigrette can be covered and refrigerated for up to 3 days.

In a large bowl, combine the lettuce, salami, chicken, provolone, tomatoes, chickpeas, basil, and Parmesan and toss lightly. Pour 1/2 cup of the dressing over the salad and add the salt and pepper. Toss well to coat, garnish with some Parmesan and serve immediately.

WHITE BALSAMIC VINAIGRETTE
Makes about 2 cups

1/2 cup white balsamic vinegar

1 egg

2 tablespoons minced shallots

2 teaspoons Dijon mustard

1 teaspoon salt

1 teaspoon freshly ground black pepper

1 cup olive oil

1 1/2 heads romaine lettuce, julienned (about 8 cups)

6 ounces hard salami, julienned (about 1 cup)

1 rotisserie chicken, meat shredded into bite-size pieces (about 3 cups)

1 cup julienned provolone cheese

1 pint grape tomatoes, halved

1 (15-ounce) can chickpeas, drained and rinsed

1 bunch basil, thinly sliced

1/2 cup shaved Parmesan cheese, plus additional for garnish

1/2 teaspoon salt

1/2 teaspoon freshly ground black pepper

FLAGSHIP SIRLOIN STEAK SALAD

Serves 4

If you're a carnivore in search of something a little lighter, here's a nice way to have your steak and eat it too. Go easy on the dressing so the greens stay fresh and crisp, and pass extra at the table for anyone who wants a little more. If you're pressed for time, you can use canned shoestring potatoes instead of fresh ones; just decrease the amount to about $^1/_4$ cup per serving. (Pictured on page 22.)

TO PREPARE THE VINAIGRETTE, combine the shallots, garlic, mustard, vinegar, roasted bell pepper, Tabasco sauce, salt, and pepper in a blender and process until smooth. With the motor running, add the olive oil. Taste and adjust the seasoning as necessary. The vinaigrette can be covered and refrigerated for up to 4 days.

TO PREPARE THE CREAM, combine all the ingredients in a small bowl and mix well. The cream can be covered and refrigerated for up to 2 days.

Preheat a gas grill to medium-high heat, prepare a fire in a charcoal grill, or place a grill pan over high heat.

Brush the onion slices on both sides with the oil and season with salt and pepper to taste.

Grill, turning once, for 1 to 2 minutes on each side, until the slices start to brown. Separate into rings and set aside.

Season both sides of the steak with salt and pepper. Place the steaks on the grill rack and cook, turning once, for 6 to 8 minutes for rare, 8 to 10 minutes for medium rare, and 10 to 12 minutes for well-done. Remove the steaks from the grill and let rest for 1 to 2 minutes to allow the juices to redistribute. Thinly slice the steak on the diagonal.

Place the greens and tomatoes in a large bowl and toss with enough of the vinaigrette to lightly coat. Season with salt and pepper to taste.

RED PEPPER–BALSAMIC VINAIGRETTE

$^1/_4$ cup chopped shallots

1 clove garlic, minced

1 tablespoon Dijon mustard

$^1/_2$ cup balsamic vinegar

$^1/_4$ cup roasted red bell peppers (see note)

$^1/_8$ teaspoon Tabasco sauce

$^1/_4$ teaspoon kosher salt

$^1/_4$ teaspoon freshly ground black pepper

$^3/_4$ cup olive oil

HORSERADISH CREAM

3 tablespoons prepared horseradish

$1^1/_2$ tablespoons thinly sliced fresh chives

1 cup sour cream

$^1/_2$ teaspoon kosher salt

$^1/_2$ teaspoon freshly ground black pepper

Divide the greens evenly among 4 plates. Top with 5 onions rings per salad and sprinkle each serving with about 2 tablespoons of the Gorgonzola cheese. Fan the steak slices over the greens and drizzle each serving with about 2 tablespoons of the horseradish cream. Top the salads with equal amounts of the shoestring potatoes and serve at once.

SHOESTRING POTATOES: Using a mandoline, julienne 1 pound russet potatoes into thin matchsticks. Rinse well in cold water and pat dry. Pour peanut oil into a heavy-bottomed pot to a depth of 2 inches and heat to 350°F. Working in batches, fry the potatoes for 2 to 4 minutes, until golden brown and crisp. Transfer with a slotted spoon to paper towels to drain. Season with salt and freshly ground black pepper. Use immediately or store for up to 24 hours in an airtight container. (Makes about 2 cups.)

ROASTED BELL PEPPERS: When roasted bell peppers are called for in this book, you can use the kind sold in jars in most supermarkets. Look for peppers packed in oil rather than vinegar, which can impart too strong a flavor. If you'd rather roast your own, preheat the broiler and line a rimmed baking sheet with aluminum foil. Place the peppers on the baking sheet and broil them, turning occasionally, for 10 to 15 minutes, until charred on all sides. Put the peppers in a plastic bag, close the bag, and let sit for 15 minutes. Remove the peppers from the bag and use a paring knife to remove the stem and seeds and scrape away the charred skin.

1 red onion, cut crosswise into $1/4$-inch slices

1 tablespoon olive oil

Salt and freshly ground black pepper

4 (6-ounce) sirloin steaks

6 cups mixed baby greens

$1/2$ pint tomatoes, halved

$1/2$ cup crumbled Gorgonzola cheese

2 cups shoestring potatoes (see note)

FINGERLING POTATOES with Sage, Blue Cheese, and Bacon

Serves 4 to 6

Appetizer or side dish? You decide. Think of this stylish small plate from Field's Lakeshore Grills as an upscale answer to potato skins. It's got something for everyone: roasted, pan-crisped fingerlings, blue cheese, and bacon, finished with fried sage leaves and ranch dressing. If you're making it for a party, you can prepare all the components ahead of time and quickly reheat just before serving.

Preheat the oven to 400°F. In a bowl, toss the potatoes with the oil and salt and pepper and spread in an even layer on a baking sheet. Roast for 20 minutes, until just cooked through. Allow to cool to room temperature. (The potatoes may be prepared to this point up to 24 hours in advance.) Slice the potatoes in half lengthwise. Maintain the oven temperature at 400°F.

Pour oil into a large, heavy-bottomed sauté pan to a depth of 3/4 inch. Place over medium-high heat until it shimmers. Add the sage leaves and fry for about 1 minute, until crisp and the oil stops bubbling. Transfer to paper towels to drain. Working in batches as necessary to avoid overcrowding, add the potatoes to the oil and cook, turning occasionally, for about 5 minutes, until golden brown on all sides. Transfer to paper towels to drain and season liberally with salt and pepper.

Place a large skillet over medium-high heat. Add the bacon and cook, turning, until crisped. Transfer to paper towels to drain and cool. Chop the bacon.

Place the potatoes cut side up in an 8 by 8-inch baking dish. Sprinkle on the bacon and then the blue cheese. Place the oven for 3 minutes to soften the cheese.

Garnish with the sage leaves and serve hot with the ranch dressing alongside for dipping.

1 pound fingerling potatoes

2 tablespoons extra virgin olive oil, plus more for frying

Salt and freshly ground black pepper

4 slices smoked bacon

12 sage leaves

1/3 cup crumbled blue cheese

1/2 cup ranch dressing, for dipping

POPOVERS

Makes 12 to 14

Welcoming guests with a basket of piping hot popovers—sometimes big and fluffy, sometimes bite-size minis—served with whipped honey butter is a long-standing tradition at many Marshall Field's restaurants. Some customers have even been known to sit down, fill up on popovers, order a cup of coffee, and ask for the check! Here's the foolproof Field's recipe for you to enjoy at home with a fancy prime-rib holiday dinner—or just a cup of coffee. If you use mini muffin tins, the baking time will be reduced; start checking for doneness after 15 minutes.

Preheat the oven to 400°F. Lightly coat popover pans or deep muffin tins with nonstick spray and heat the pans in the oven for at least 15 minutes.

Crack the eggs into a bowl and beat using an electric mixer until frothy. Add the milk and butter and mix well. Add the flour and salt and mix just to combine.

Divide the batter among the preheated pans, filling each cup just under half full. Bake for 30 to 40 minutes, until puffy and well browned. Remove from the pan and serve warm. The finished popovers should should pull away from the pan easily and feel light to the touch.

WHIPPED HONEY BUTTER: In a bowl, whip $1/2$ pound butter and 2 tablespoons honey using an electric mixer until light and fluffy.

5 large eggs

$1^2/3$ cups whole milk

5 tablespoons unsalted butter, melted

$1^2/3$ cups all-purpose flour

$1/2$ teaspoon salt

COCONUT SHRIMP with Mango-Pineapple Sauce

Serves 4 to 6

Crispy coconut-crusted shrimp make a pretty irresistible hors d'oeuvre or first course, especially when you pair them with a sweet-spicy tropical dipping sauce. To serve these as a passed finger food, deep-fry them before the guests arrive and keep them warm for up to half an hour in a 200°F oven. The dipping sauce also makes a great low-fat salad dressing.

TO PREPARE THE SAUCE, combine the mango, pineapple, ginger, chile paste, lime juice, and sesame oil in a blender or food processor. Blend on high speed to a smooth purée. Season to taste with salt and pepper.

Combine the breadcrumbs and coconut in a small bowl. Pour the flour into a separate small bowl. Pat the shrimp dry and season liberally on both sides with salt and pepper. One at a time, toss the shrimp in the flour and shake off the excess. Dip into the egg wash and then into the coconut mixture.

Pour the peanut oil into a heavy-bottomed saucepan to a depth of 1 inch. Place over medium-high heat until it reaches 350°F. (If you don't have a deep-fat thermometer, test the temperature by putting a cube of bread in the oil; it should take about 1 minute to brown.) Working in batches, add the shrimp and fry for 2 minutes on each side, until golden brown and cooked through. Using tongs or a slotted spoon, transfer to paper towels to drain.

Arrange the shrimp on individual plates or a platter and serve hot with the sauce alongside for dipping.

MANGO-PINEAPPLE SAUCE

1/2 cup diced fresh mango

1 cup diced fresh pineapple

2 teaspoons minced fresh ginger

1/2 teaspoon sambal oelek chile paste (see page 36)

1 1/2 teaspoons freshly squeezed lime juice

1/2 teaspoon sesame oil

Salt and freshly ground black pepper

1/2 cup Japanese breadcrumbs (panko)

1 cup sweetened shredded coconut

1/2 cup all-purpose flour

26 large (21 to 25 count) shrimp, peeled and deveined, tail on

2 eggs whisked with 1 tablespoon water

Peanut oil, for frying

SHRIMP SALAD SANDWICH on Toasted Cheese Bread

Serves 4

Years ago, someone in the kitchens of Field's Detroit restaurant (which was then a part of Hudson's) came up with the idea of serving a classic bay shrimp salad on toasted cheese bread. It's one of those simple combinations that never goes out of style. Look for cheddar cheese bread at your local bakery, or try toasted egg bread or soft Asiago bread.

Combine the shrimp, celery, green onions, mayonnaise, mustard, lemon juice, salt, and pepper in a large bowl and mix well. Taste and adjust the seasoning as necessary. Use immediately or cover and refrigerate for up to 2 days.

Toast the bread slices. Spread half of the slices with butter. Arrange a lettuce leaf on each buttered slice of bread. Top each lettuce leaf with one-quarter of the shrimp salad. Lightly spread the remaining pieces of bread with mayonnaise and place on top of the sandwiches. Serve immediately.

1 pound cooked shrimp, chopped

1 cup finely diced celery

2 green onions, thinly sliced

1/2 cup mayonnaise, plus more for spreading

1/4 cup honey mustard

1 teaspoon freshly squeezed lemon juice

1 teaspoon salt

1/2 teaspoon freshly ground black pepper

8 slices cheddar cheese bread

Butter, for spreading

4 leaves green leaf lettuce

NEW ORLEANS–STYLE BARBECUED SHRIMP

Serves 4 | *Roll up your sleeves and prepare to be wowed. These popular peel-and-eat shrimp in a buttery Creole BBQ sauce are messy in the best way. Serve them with rice pilaf, ice cold beer, and plenty of moist towels.*

TO PREPARE THE SEASONING, combine all the ingredients in a small bowl and mix well. The seasoning should be stored in an airtight container.

Combine 4 teaspoons of the Creole seasoning, the Worcestershire sauce, wine, lemon juice, pepper, and garlic in a large saucepan over medium-high heat. Add the shrimp and cook, stirring occasionally, for about 3 minutes, until the shrimp begin to turn pink. Slowly swirl in the butter, one cube at a time, and continue to stir the shrimp for about 5 minutes, until the sauce has thickened and the shrimp are cooked through.

Divide the shrimp and sauce among 4 warmed bowls. Serve immediately with the bread for sopping up all of the decadent sauce.

CREOLE SEASONING

$1^1/_2$ tablespoons paprika

2 teaspoons freshly ground black pepper

$1^1/_2$ teaspoons kosher salt

1 teaspoon garlic powder

1 teaspoon dried thyme

1 teaspoon dried basil

1 teaspoon onion powder

$^3/_4$ teaspoon ground cayenne pepper

6 tablespoons Worcestershire sauce

$^1/_4$ cup dry white wine

2 tablespoons freshly squeezed lemon juice

1 tablespoon plus 1 teaspoon freshly ground black pepper

2 teaspoons minced garlic

24 ounces jumbo shrimp, shells on

1 cup cold unsalted butter, cut into cubes

Sliced French bread, for serving

ALMOND-CRUSTED WALLEYE SANDWICH

Serves 4

Walleye is the state fish of Minnesota, and this sandwich made its menu debut at Field's in Minneapolis. To bone a walleye fillet, find the row of pin bones and make two long cuts on either side to create a V-shaped wedge, which you can then remove and discard. If walleye is not available, tilapia or trout make good substitutes. This dish works beautifully as an entrée—just skip the lettuce and bread.

TO PREPARE THE SAUCE, combine the tarragon, capers, mayonnaise, lemon juice, salt, pepper, and Tabasco sauce in the bowl of a food processor. Blend to combine. Transfer to a bowl and fold in the red peppers. Taste and adjust the seasoning with salt and pepper as necessary. The sauce can be covered and refrigerated for up to 3 days.

Combine the almonds and breadcrumbs in the bowl of a food processor. Pulse until chopped and combined but not finely ground. Transfer to a shallow bowl. Pour the milk in another shallow bowl.

Season the fish on both sides with the salt and pepper. Dip in the milk then roll in the almond breading, coating all sides evenly. Place a large, nonstick skillet over medium-high heat and add the oil. When the oil is hot, add the fish in batches if necessary to avoid crowding, and cook, turning once, for 3 to 4 minutes on each side, until the breading is golden and the fish is cooked through.

Place 1 piece of fish on the bottom half of each roll. Top with a spoonful of the tartar sauce and some lettuce. Cover with the top half of the roll and serve with a lemon wedge on the side.

LEMON-CAPER TARTAR SAUCE

2 tablespoons chopped fresh tarragon leaves

2 tablespoons drained capers

1 cup mayonnaise

1 tablespoon freshly squeezed lemon juice

1/2 teaspoon salt

1/2 teaspoon freshly ground black pepper

Dash of Tabasco sauce

2 tablespoons finely diced roasted red bell pepper (see page 45)

1/2 cup sliced almonds, toasted (see page 32)

1/2 cup Japanese breadcrumbs (panko)

1/2 cup milk

1/2 teaspoon salt

1/2 teaspoon freshly ground black pepper

4 (6-ounce) pieces walleye, skin and bones removed

1/4 cup vegetable oil

4 sandwich rolls

1 cup shredded romaine lettuce

4 lemon wedges

SEARED HALIBUT with Asparagus Sauce

Serves 4

Asparagus is a spring thing. So is halibut. Corporate Executive Chef Tim Scott came up with this novel way to combine them for a spring menu at the Walnut Room. The asparagus is cooked quickly in broth to retain its bright green color, then puréed to make a fresh, flavorful sauce.

TO PREPARE THE SAUCE, heat 1 tablespoon of the butter in a heavy saucepan over medium-high heat. Add the onion and garlic and sauté for about 1 minute, stirring occasionally, until soft. Add the asparagus and the broth. Simmer until tender, 5 to 7 minutes. Be careful not to over-cook the asparagus; it should still be bright green. Reserve a few of the tips for garnish.

Transfer to a blender, add the parsley, and blend until smooth. Add the remaining tablespoon of butter, Tabasco sauce, and a pinch each of salt and pepper and blend again. It should be the consistency of a thick cream soup; if it is too thick add a little more broth. Keep warm. (The sauce can also be made ahead and reheated.)

Season the fish liberally on both sides with salt and pepper. Heat the olive oil in a large sauté pan over medium-high heat until it shimmers, Add the fish and cook, turning once, for 3 to 5 minutes on each side, until the fish is cooked through (if the fish fillets are very thick, you may need to place the pan in a 375°F oven to finish cooking).

Drizzle fish with the warm asparagus sauce and garnish with the reserved asparagus tips.

ASPARAGUS SAUCE

2 tablespoons unsalted butter

1/2 small onion, coarsely chopped (about 1/2 cup)

1 teaspoon minced garlic

1 bunch asparagus, trimmed and cut into 2-inch lengths

1 1/2 cups chicken or vegetable broth, plus more if needed

1 teaspoon chopped fresh parsley

Dash of Tabasco sauce (optional)

Salt and freshly ground black pepper

4 (6 to 8-ounce) halibut fillets

1 tablespoon extra virgin olive oil

ROASTED PORK with Maple Mashed Sweet Potatoes

Serves 6 to 8

This recipe uses the signature brining method from the Lakeshore Grills that makes the meat juicy and perfectly seasoned all the way through. A bone-in roast is too spectacular not to show off. For full dramatic effect, present it whole and slice it into individual chops at the table.

In a very large bowl or cooler, combine the water, sugar, salt, and pepper and stir to dissolve the sugar and salt. Completely submerge the pork in the brine. Cover and refrigerate for at least 12 hours or up to 36 hours.

Preheat the oven to 275°F. Combine the garlic, rosemary, parsley, and olive oil in a food processor and blend to a paste. Remove the pork from the brine and gently pat dry with paper towels. Season with salt and rub the garlic-herb paste all over the pork. Place the pork, bone side up, on a rack fitted over a roasting pan. Roast for $1^1/_2$ hours, until the pork reaches an internal temperature of 130°F. Increase the oven temperature to 425°F degrees and roast an additional 20 minutes, until the pork reaches 145°F. Remove from the oven and allow to rest for 10 minutes before carving into individual chops.

TO PREPARE THE CHUTNEY, combine all the ingredients in a saucepan over medium heat. Bring to a boil then decrease the heat to a simmer and cook, stirring occasionally, for 30 minutes, until thick. Remove the cinnamon sticks. Serve the chutney warm or allow to cool to room temperature, cover, and refrigerate for up to 1 week.

TO PREPARE THE SWEET POTATOES, place the potatoes in a large saucepan of well-salted water to cover. Bring to a boil over high heat and cook for about 20 minutes, until tender. Drain the sweet potatoes and return to the pan. Add the butter, syrup, salt, and pepper and mash with a potato masher or heavy wire whisk until smooth. Taste and adjust the seasoning as necessary. Serve immediately or allow to cool to room temperature, cover, and refrigerate for up to 2 days.

Place a pork chop on each plate and serve with the chutney and sweet potatoes.

1 gallon water

1 cup packed brown sugar

1 cup kosher salt

$^1/_2$ cup ground black pepper

1 (8-rib) pork loin rack, bones frenched

$^1/_4$ cup garlic cloves

$^1/_4$ cup fresh rosemary leaves

$^1/_4$ cup fresh flat-leaf parsley

2 tablespoons extra virgin olive oil

APPLE-CRANBERRY CHUTNEY

$^1/_2$ red onion, diced (about $^1/_2$ cup)

1 tablespoon ground ginger

1 cup apple cider vinegar

1 cup freshly squeezed orange juice

$^3/_4$ cup packed brown sugar

$^1/_2$ cup light corn syrup

2 cinnamon sticks

2 Braeburn apples, peeled and diced

$^3/_4$ cup dried cranberries

$^3/_4$ cup thinly sliced dried apricots

MAPLE MASHED SWEET POTATOES

2 pounds sweet potatoes, peeled and cut into large chunks

4 tablespoons unsalted butter

2 tablespoons pure maple syrup

1 teaspoon salt

1 teaspoon freshly ground black pepper

THAI CHICKEN STIR-FRY SALAD

Serves 4

If you like the fun and drama of tostada salad, try this East-meets-West, salad-meets-entrée version that's the signature dish of the 700 Express Restaurant at the downtown Minneapolis Marshall Field's. It's brown rice and a full-flavored chicken and vegetable stir-fry, mounded dramatically in a crispy egg roll skin cup—all drizzled with a creamy Thai peanut dressing.

Preheat the oven to 350°F.

TO PREPARE THE SAUCE, combine the sugar, sesame seeds, soy sauce, sesame seed oil, garlic, chile paste, and tamarind paste in a small saucepan and bring to a boil over high heat. Remove from the heat and immediately stir in the green onions. The sauce can be covered and refrigerated for up to 5 days.

TO PREPARE THE DRESSING, combine ¹/₄ cup of the Thai sauce, the cilantro, peanut butter, and vinegar in a bowl. Whisk until thoroughly combined. Whisking constantly, add the oil in a slow, steady stream to make an emulsion.

Arrange the egg roll skins in 4 cups of a nonstick muffin tin (don't let the edges touch each other) and press down on the centers to form bowls. Brush the top surfaces very lightly with vegetable oil and bake for 15 minutes, until crisp and golden.

Bring a small saucepan full of water to a boil over high heat. Fill a bowl with ice water. Submerge the broccoli in the boiling water for 1 minute, until it turns bright green. Immediately drain and place into the ice water. Drain again.

Place a large, deep skillet or wok over high heat and add the oil. When the oil is hot, add the chicken and cook for 5 minutes, until almost done. Add the broccoli, asparagus, carrots, and bell pepper and cook for 3 to 4 minutes, until the chicken is cooked through. Add the rice and ¹/₂ cup of the Thai sauce and stir until thoroughly heated. Season with the salt and pepper.

THAI SAUCE

¹/₂ cup sugar

3 teaspoons sesame seeds

1 cup soy sauce

2 teaspoons sesame seed oil

3 tablespoons minced garlic

2 tablespoons sambal oelek chile paste (see page 36)

2 tablespoons tamarind paste

1 cup thinly sliced green onions

THAI PEANUT DRESSING

1 tablespoon chopped cilantro

3 tablespoons peanut butter

¹/₄ cup white vinegar

¹/₂ cup vegetable oil

4 egg roll skins

³/₄ cup broccoli florets

¹/₄ cup vegetable oil

4 boneless skinless chicken breasts, cut into ¹/₄-inch strips

³/₄ cup asparagus, cut into 2-inch lengths

³/₄ cup julienned carrots

¹/₂ cup julienned red bell pepper

3 cups cooked brown rice

¹/₂ teaspoon kosher salt

To serve, divide the lettuce between 4 plates. Place the egg roll bowls on top of the lettuce. Divide the chicken and rice mixture equally among the bowls. Drizzle each serving with ¼ cup of the peanut dressing, garnish with the green onions, and serve immediately.

½ teaspoon freshly ground black pepper

2 romaine lettuce hearts, chopped

¼ cup green onions, thinly sliced on the diagonal, for garnish

ROASTED GARLIC CHICKEN

Serves 4 | *An overnight soak in a roasted garlic and lemon brine gives the renowned rotisserie chickens at Marshall Field's Lakeshore Grills their moist, tender texture and delicately sweet garlic flavor. Here's how to turn out a crisp-skinned, juicy version at home.*

TO PREPARE THE BRINE, combine the garlic, water, salt, pepper, and olive oil in a blender and purée until smooth. Squeeze in the juice from the lemon wedges, reserving the rinds, and blend to combine. Stir in the bay leaves.

Place the chicken in a large resealable plastic bag or a bowl. Pour the brine over the chicken and toss to coat. Add the lemon rinds and press the air out of the bag and seal tightly or cover the bowl with plastic wrap. Refrigerate for 12 to 24 hours.

Preheat the oven to 375°F. Remove the chicken from the brine. Season liberally on all sides with salt and pepper. Place the chicken, breast side up, on a rack set in a roasting pan. Roast for about 1 hour, until the juices run clear from the thigh when pierced with a fork.

Let the chicken rest for 10 minutes, then cut it into portions and serve hot.

ROASTING GARLIC: Preheat the oven to 400°F. Place $1/2$ cup peeled garlic cloves in the center of a piece of aluminum foil. Sprinkle $1/2$ teaspoon extra virgin olive oil over the cloves and fold the foil over to form a loose packet. Place the packet on a baking sheet and roast for 30 to 40 minutes, until the garlic is very soft and light brown. Allow to cool before using.

ROASTED GARLIC–LEMON BRINE

$1/2$ cup roasted garlic cloves (see note)

2 cups water

1 tablespoon salt

$1/2$ teaspoon freshly ground black pepper

1 tablespoon extra virgin olive oil

$1/2$ lemon, cut into 4 wedges

2 bay leaves, crushed

1 (3 to 4-pound) whole roasting chicken

ASIAGO-CRUSTED CHICKEN with Mustard-Glazed Carrots

Serves 4

A Walnut Room favorite, second in popularity only to Mrs. Hering's Famous Chicken Potpie (page 65), these golden-brown chicken cutlets are easy enough to be a midweek mainstay and elegant enough to serve at a dinner party. The sweet mustard-glazed carrots are a snap, too—no chopping necessary! Serve buttery mashed potatoes on the side to recreate the full Walnut Room experience.

TO PREPARE THE CARROTS, in a large sauté pan, combine the carrots, water, butter, olive oil, sugar, and mustard over medium heat. Bring to a boil, then decrease the heat and simmer, stirring often, for 8 to 12 minutes, until the water has evaporated and the carrots are coated with a glaze. Check the carrots for doneness; if they are not tender, add a little more water and cook for a few minutes more. Season with the salt and pepper and sprinkle with the chives.

TO PREPARE THE SAUCE, pour the cream into a small saucepan over medium heat and bring to a boil. Stir in the mustard, salt, and pepper and decrease the heat to a simmer. Cook, stirring occasionally, for 10 to 15 minutes, until reduced by half. The sauce should coat the back of a spoon. Taste and adjust the seasoning as necessary.

TO PREPARE CHICKEN, place the cheese and breadcrumbs in a food processor and pulse to combine. Transfer to a shallow bowl and stir in the parsley. Pour the flour onto a plate. Whisk the egg and water together in a separate shallow bowl.

Liberally season the chicken breasts on both sides with salt and pepper. Dredge in the flour and shake off any excess. Dip in the egg wash, then coat on all sides with the Asiago breadcrumbs.

Place a large, nonstick sauté pan over medium-high heat and add the oil. When the oil shimmers, add the chicken and cook, turning once, for 4 to 5 minutes on each side, until golden brown on the outside and no longer pink on the inside.

Serve immediately, accompanied by the carrots and mustard sauce.

MUSTARD-GLAZED CARROTS

1 pound baby carrots

1 cup water

1 tablespoon unsalted butter

1 tablespoon olive oil

2 tablespoons brown sugar

1¹/₂ tablespoons Dijon mustard

1¹/₂ teaspoons salt

¹/₂ teaspoon freshly ground black pepper

2 tablespoons chopped fresh chives

POMMERY MUSTARD SAUCE

1¹/₂ cups heavy cream

¹/₄ cup whole grain mustard

¹/₂ teaspoon salt

¹/₂ teaspoon freshly ground black pepper

CHICKEN

³/₄ cup shredded Asiago cheese

¹/₄ cup Japanese breadcrumbs (panko)

1 tablespoon chopped fresh flat-leaf parsley

¹/₂ cup all-purpose flour

1 egg

2 tablespoons water

4 boneless skinless chicken breast halves

1¹/₂ teaspoons salt

1¹/₂ teaspoons freshly ground black pepper

¹/₄ cup olive oil

MRS. HERING'S FAMOUS CHICKEN POTPIE

Serves 6

This is it! The pie that started it all back in 1890 and went on to become the culinary icon of Marshall Field's. If you're longing to experience the great American chicken potpie, made from scratch with a whole chicken, topped with a flaky, hand-rolled crust, you'll love Mrs. Hering's recipe. And you won't be alone. During the holiday season, the Walnut Room serves thirty-five hundred of her famous pies a week.

Combine the chicken, carrot, celery, onion, and salt in a large stockpot. Add cold water just to cover and bring to a boil over high heat. Decrease the heat to low and simmer for 45 minutes. Transfer the chicken to a plate and allow to cool. Increase the heat to high and boil for 20 minutes to concentrate the broth. Strain the broth through a fine-mesh sieve and discard the vegetables. When cool enough to handle, pull the chicken meat from the bones and shred into bite-size pieces.

TO PREPARE THE DOUGH, combine the flour, salt, and butter in the bowl of a food processor and pulse 5 times to combine. Add the shortening and pulse a few more times, until the dough resembles coarse cornmeal. Transfer to a bowl and sprinkle with 3 tablespoons of the ice water. Stir and then press together with a wooden spoon until the dough sticks together. A little at a time, add more water if the dough won't come together. Shape the dough into a ball and then flatten into a disk. Cover in plastic wrap and refrigerate for at least 30 minutes or up to 2 days before rolling.

Preheat the oven to 400°F. Place a large saucepan over medium heat and add the butter. When the butter is melted, add the onion, carrots, and celery and cook, stirring occasionally, for 10 minutes, until the onion is soft and translucent. Add the flour and cook, stirring, for 1 minute. Slowly whisk in the milk and 2½ cups of the chicken broth. Decrease the heat to low and simmer, stirring often, for 10 minutes. Add the chicken meat, thyme, sherry, peas, parsley, salt, and pepper and stir well. Taste and adjust the seasoning as necessary. Divide the warm filling among six 10- or 12-ounce potpie tins or individual ramekins.

continued

1 (3½-pound) frying chicken

1 carrot

1 celery stalk

1 small onion, halved

2 teaspoons salt

PIE DOUGH

1½ cups all-purpose flour

½ teaspoon salt

½ cup cold unsalted butter, diced

¼ cup vegetable shortening, chilled

3 to 4 tablespoons ice water

6 tablespoons unsalted butter

1 large onion, diced (about 1¼ cups)

3 carrots, thinly sliced on the diagonal

3 celery stalks, thinly sliced on the diagonal

½ cup all-purpose flour

1½ cups milk

1 teaspoon chopped fresh thyme leaves

¼ cup dry sherry

¾ cup frozen green peas, thawed

2 tablespoons minced fresh parsley

2 teaspoons salt

½ teaspoon freshly ground black pepper

1 egg whisked with 1 tablespoon water

Place the dough on a floured surface and roll out to ¹/₄ inch thick. Cut into 6 rounds about 1 inch larger than the dish circumference. Lay a dough round over each potpie filling. Tuck the overhanging dough back under itself and flute the edges with a fork. Cut a 1-inch slit in the top of each pie. Brush the tops of the pies with the egg wash.

Line a baking sheet with aluminum foil. Place the pies on the baking sheet and bake for 25 minutes, until the pastry is golden and the filling is bubbling. Serve hot.

MUSHROOM-CRUSTED SIRLOIN STEAK

Serves 6 | *Want to turn out restaurant caliber steaks? Dust the meat with ground dried mushrooms before grilling. Once you discover this magic powder, you'll find you can use it on pork, lamb, poultry, and seafood too. It seals in the juices and creates a tasty crust on whatever you're grilling or pan-searing. Mashed potatoes and sautéed spinach make the perfect accompaniments for this hearty entrée.*

Place the dried mushrooms in a blender or spice grinder and process to a powder. Transfer to a shallow bowl or plate.

Preheat a gas grill to medium-high or prepare a hot fire in a charcoal grill. Season the steaks liberally on both sides with salt and pepper. Dip the steaks into the mushroom powder to coat on both sides. Grill the steaks, turning once, for 8 to 14 minutes, to desired doneness.

Place a large sauté pan over high heat and add 4 tablespoons of the butter. When the butter melts, add the fresh mushrooms, thyme, garlic, 1 teaspoon salt, and $1/2$ teaspoon pepper. Do not toss. Sear the mushrooms for about 3 minutes, until they are well browned on one side. Toss and cook for 3 minutes, until well browned and caramelized all over. Remove from the heat and stir in the remaining 2 tablespoons butter, truffle oil, and parsley. Taste and adjust the seasoning as necessary.

Place a steak on each plate and top with a generous portion of the mushrooms. Serve at once.

$3/4$ ounce dried porcini or other wild mushrooms

6 (1-inch-thick) sirloin steaks

1 teaspoon salt, plus more for seasoning

$1/2$ teaspoon freshly ground black pepper, plus more for seasoning

6 tablespoons unsalted butter

1 pound mixed wild fresh mushrooms, sliced

2 teaspoons chopped fresh thyme leaves

2 teaspoons minced garlic

2 teaspoons truffle or porcini oil

1 tablespoon chopped fresh flat-leaf parsley

OVEN-BAKED MEATLOAF

Serves 4 to 6

A Marshall Field's classic for decades, this meatloaf gets its big personality from a few special Mediterranean-inspired accents: pesto, pine nuts, garlic croutons, and fresh spinach. Serve it with mashed potatoes and brown gravy mixed, Field's-style, with some diced roasted red bell peppers. And be sure to save a slice or two to make yourself an amazing meatloaf sandwich for lunch the next day.

Preheat the oven to 350°F. Combine the croutons and broth in a small bowl and set aside to soak for 10 minutes. Place a sauté pan over medium-high heat and add the oil. Add the onion and sauté for 7 to 8 minutes, until translucent.

Beat the eggs in a large bowl. Add the pesto, pine nuts, Worcestershire sauce, salt, and pepper and mix well. Add the crouton mixture, onion, ground steak, and spinach. Mix with your hands until just combined. Pat the mixture into a standard loaf pan (about 4¹/₂ by 9 inches). Place on a baking sheet and bake for 1 hour and 15 minutes, until cooked through. Let stand for 10 minutes before slicing and serving with a generous drizzle of gravy atop each slice.

TOASTING PINE NUTS: Preheat the oven to 325°F. Spread the pine nuts on a baking sheet and bake, shaking the pan occasionally, for 4 to 7 minutes, until golden brown. Set a kitchen timer and keep a constant eye on the pine nuts as they toast, because they burn easily.

RED PEPPER GRAVY: In a saucepan, over medium heat, combine 1 cup brown sauce or gravy and 2 tablespoons finely diced roasted red peppers. Simmer for a few minutes. Season to taste with salt and pepper.

4 ounces store-bought or homemade garlic croutons, crushed

1 cup beef broth

1 tablespoon extra virgin olive oil

1 yellow onion, finely chopped

2 large eggs

2¹/₂ tablespoons prepared pesto

2¹/₂ tablespoons pine nuts, toasted (see note)

1¹/₂ teaspoons Worcestershire sauce

1 teaspoon salt

¹/₂ teaspoon freshly ground black pepper

2 pounds ground round steak

1¹/₂ cups julienned fresh spinach

Red pepper gravy, for serving (see note)

INDIVIDUAL APPLE STRUDELS

Serves 6 | *Strudel might sound intimidating, but this version, made with store-bought puff pastry, an easy apple-cranberry filling, and a quick streusel topping, isn't tricky at all. At Field's, strudels like these are an annual Oktoberfest tradition. Serve them with a scoop of good vanilla ice cream and a drizzle of warm caramel sauce. Or try toasted pecan ice cream, chef Tim Scott's favorite accompaniment.*

TO PREPARE THE TOPPING, combine all the ingredients in a small bowl and mix together with a fork until crumbly.

Combine the apples, cranberries, sugar, butter, cinnamon stick, water, and nutmeg in a large sauté pan over medium-high heat. Cook, stirring frequently, for 10 to 12 minutes, until the apples are softened. Remove from the heat and stir in the walnuts. Allow to cool to room temperature or cover and refrigerate for up to 2 days.

Preheat the oven to 425°F. Cut each of the puff pastry sheets into 4 equal squares (reserve 2 squares for another use). Using your hands, stretch the squares about $1/2$ inch larger in each direction. Whisk together the egg and water in a small bowl. Using a pastry brush, brush the pastry squares with the egg wash. Place $1/2$ cup of the apple filling in the middle of each square. Fold the corners over partway to make a hexagonal pastry, covering part of the filling but leaving most of it exposed. Press down lightly. Brush the folded-over corners with the egg wash and sprinkle with sugar. Sprinkle 1 tablespoon of the topping over the filling.

Line 2 baking sheets with parchment paper. Using a wide spatula, carefully transfer the pastries to the prepared baking sheets, leaving space between them. Bake for 30 minutes, until the pastry is puffed and golden. Serve warm.

STREUSEL TOPPING

$1/4$ cup all-purpose flour

3 tablespoons sugar

2 tablespoons unsalted butter

$3^1/2$ cups peeled sliced Granny Smith apples

$1/2$ cup dried cranberries

$1/4$ cup sugar, plus more for sprinkling

4 tablespoons unsalted butter

1 cinnamon stick

2 tablespoons water

$1/4$ teaspoon ground nutmeg

1 cup walnuts, toasted and chopped (see page 32)

2 sheets frozen puff pastry dough, thawed

1 egg

1 tablespoon water

CRANBERRY-CAMPARI POACHED PEARS

Serves 6 | *The next time you're looking for an elegant make-ahead dessert, consider these pears poached in cranberry juice and Campari and filled with creamy orange-scented mascarpone cheese. The crimson fruit and sauce, snowy white filling, and bright green mint leaf make this a particularly good choice as the finale of a holiday meal.*

Combine the cranberry juice, orange juice, sugar, Campari, cinnamon stick, and orange peel in a large, heavy saucepan over high heat. Bring to a boil, stirring until the sugar dissolves. Cover, decrease the heat to low, and keep warm while you prepare the pears.

Peel the pears, leaving the stems attached. Cut a thin slice off of the bottom of each pear so that it will stand upright. Using melon baller, core the pears from the bottom, leaving the stems intact. Stand the pears upright in the poaching liquid and increase the heat to medium-low. Simmer uncovered for about 20 minutes, until the pears are tender when pierced with the tip of a knife. Remove from the heat and allow the pears to cool in the poaching liquid. Refrigerate them in the poaching liquid until cold, at least 6 hours.

TO PREPARE THE SAUCE, combine the raspberries with their syrup and the liqueur in a blender and purée. Pass the purée through a fine-mesh sieve. Refrigerate until cold, about 1 hour. (The pears and raspberry sauce can be stored in separate covered containers in the refrigerator for up to 1 day.)

Combine the mascarpone, confectioners' sugar, liqueur, and orange zest in a bowl and whisk to blend. Fill each pear's cavity with the mascarpone mixture.

Spoon a pool of the raspberry sauce onto each plate. Stand the pears upright in the center of the sauce. Using a vegetable peeler, shave curls of the chocolate over each serving, and garnish each plate with a mint leaf. Serve at once.

2 cups cranberry juice

1 cup freshly squeezed orange juice

1^1/$_2$ cups sugar

^{1}/$_2$ cup Campari

1 cinnamon stick

Peel of 1 orange

6 (7-ounce) Bosc pears

RASPBERRY SAUCE

1 (10-ounce) package frozen
  raspberries in syrup, thawed

2 tablespoons orange liqueur

1 cup mascarpone cheese or softened
  cream cheese

3 tablespoons confectioners' sugar

2 tablespoons orange liqueur

1 teaspoon finely grated orange zest

1 (4-ounce) bar white chocolate,
  for shavings

Fresh mint leaves, for garnish

For Here or To Go

You shop, you get hungry, you want a little something. Long before food courts and fast food, Marshall Field's understood the idea offering a quick bite or light lunch right in the store.

The tearooms led the way, starting in the 1890s. In the 1950s, the Pantry, an epicurean market, was decades ahead of its time in luring guests with hard-to-find gourmet foods and ingredients, offering everything from Field's famed Thousand Island Dressing to Stasbourg pâté de foie gras, wild boar and rattlesnake meat, eighteen varieties of honey, and even Mexican fried worms.

Three decades later, the popular Marketplace Foods took up where the Pantry left off, offering home-style comfort food, sandwiches, salads, sushi, pizza, and deli fare, as well as a selection of Field's own specialty foods products. The Thousand Island Dressing is still available, though worms are no longer on the menu. Here are recipes for four all-time favorite salads from Marketplace to enjoy at home.

BLUEBERRY CHICKEN SALAD
with Apples, Grapes, Hazelnuts, and Blue Cheese

Serves 6

You might not think of combining blueberries and chicken, but judging by the popularity of this salad, it's a happy match. This makes a nice main dish for a summertime picnic, when blueberries are at their best.

In a small bowl, whisk together the mustard, shallot, honey, lime juice, salt, pepper, and rosemary. Slowly whisk in the olive oil to make an emulsion.

In a large bowl, combine the chicken, apple, grapes, blueberries, hazelnuts, and blue cheese and toss well.

Pour the dressing over the salad and toss well to coat thoroughly. Taste and adjust the seasoning as necessary. Serve immediately or cover and refrigerate for up to 2 days.

2 teaspoons Dijon mustard

2 tablespoons minced shallot

2 tablespoons honey

3 tablespoons freshly squeezed lime juice

1 teaspoon salt

$1/2$ teaspoon freshly ground black pepper

1 tablespoon minced fresh rosemary leaves

$1/4$ cup olive oil

1 roasted chicken, meat torn into bite-size pieces (about 3 cups)

1 large Granny Smith apple, cut into $1/4$-inch slices

$1 1/2$ cups green grapes

$1 1/2$ cups blueberries, picked over

$1/2$ cup hazelnuts, toasted, skinned, and coarsely chopped (see page 98)

$1/2$ cup crumbled blue cheese

FIELD'S | MARKETPLACE™

TWISTED TUNA SALAD

Serves 6 | *Okay, the only thing twisted about this salad is the rotini pasta. In fact, it's classic deli comfort food— tuna, pasta, and peas in a creamy buttermilk dressing. This was one of the original Marketplace salads back in the early eighties and it's still one of the most popular lunchtime items.*

Bring a pot of salted water to a boil over high heat. Add the pasta and cook according to the package instructions, until al dente. Drain, rinse with cool water, and drain again thoroughly.

In a large bowl, combine the pasta, tuna, celery, onion, and peas and toss well. In a separate bowl, whisk together the sugar, salt, pepper, buttermilk, and mayonnaise. Pour the dressing over the salad and toss well to coat thoroughly. Serve immediately or cover and refrigerate for up to 3 days.

1 pound rotini pasta

2 (12-ounce) cans tuna packed in water, drained

1^1/$_4$ cups diced celery

^{1}/$_2$ cup minced red onion

1 pound frozen peas, thawed and drained

2 tablespoons sugar

2 teaspoons salt

2 teaspoons freshly ground black pepper

1^1/$_2$ cups buttermilk

^{1}/$_2$ cup mayonnaise

LEELANAU TURKEY SALAD

Serves 6

Corporate Executive Chef Elizabeth Brown created this crowd-pleasing salad of smoked turkey and dried cherries and named it after the cherry capital of the world, Leelenau County in Michigan, where she and her family spend their summers. Serve a scoop over mixed greens or pile it on hearty wheat bread for a memorable sandwich.

In a large bowl, combine the turkey, celery, cherries, walnuts, green onions, and parsley and toss well. In a separate bowl, whisk together the mayonnaise, sour cream, Gorgonzola, salt, and pepper. Pour the dressing over the salad and toss well to coat thoroughly. Taste and adjust the seasoning as necessary. Serve immediately or cover and refrigerate for up to 3 days.

2 pounds smoked turkey breast or leftover roast turkey, diced

1 1/2 cups thinly sliced celery

1 1/4 cups dried tart cherries

1 cup walnuts, toasted and chopped (see page 32)

1/2 cup thinly sliced green onions

1 tablespoon chopped fresh flat-leaf parsley

3/4 cup light mayonnaise

3/4 cup sour cream

4 ounces Gorgonzola cheese, crumbled

1/2 teaspoon salt

1 teaspoon freshly ground black pepper

ORIENTAL CHICKEN PASTA SALAD

Serves 4 to 6 | *This salad has been among the top sellers at Marketplace for years. You can make it with left-over cooked chicken or use the oven-poaching method from the White Meat Chicken Salad recipe (page 39), as the Marketplace chefs do. The creamy sesame dressing is also good on an Asian-style napa cabbage slaw or as a table sauce for grilled shrimp, steak, chicken, or pork.*

TO PREPARE THE DRESSING, combine the egg yolk, soy sauce, vinegar, and sugar in a food processor. Blend to combine. With the motor running, add the oils in a slow, steady stream to make an emulsion. Stir in the pepper and taste and adjust the seasoning as necessary. Use immediately or cover and refrigerate for up to 2 days.

Bring a pot of salted water to a boil over high heat. Add the pasta and cook according to the package instructions, until al dente. Drain, rinse with cool water, and drain again thoroughly.

Bring a small saucepan of water to a boil over high heat. Fill a bowl with ice water. Submerge the snow peas in the boiling water for no more than 1 minute, until they turn bright green. Immediately drain and place into the ice water. Drain again, then slice the snow peas on the diagonal into long strips.

In a large bowl, combine the pasta, snow peas, chicken, green onions, and mushrooms and toss well. Pour 1 cup of the dressing over the salad and toss well to coat thoroughly. Cover and refrigerate until chilled before serving.

CREAMY SESAME DRESSING
Makes about 2 cups

1 egg yolk

1/4 cup soy sauce

1/4 cup rice vinegar

1/4 cup sugar

1 1/4 cups vegetable oil

1/4 cup sesame oil

1/4 teaspoon freshly ground black pepper

8 ounces fusilli pasta

1 cup snow peas

2 cups shredded cooked chicken

4 green onions, thinly sliced

1 1/2 cups thinly sliced button mushrooms

FRANGO
CHOCOLATES

Field's, Frederick's and Frango—A Meeting of the Mints

Marshall Field's 1929 purchase of the Seattle-based Frederick and Nelson Company was a sweet deal in more ways than one. With that department store came the secret recipe for what would become one of the most famous candies in the world. Frango started out as a dessert, a frozen ice cream–like confection with a flaky texture, served at Frederick and Nelson. Eventually, pies and fountain drinks were added to the Frango line, and in 1918 the company hired a renowned candymaker to create a chocolate mint Frango truffle.

As soon as the store's purchase went through, Frederick and Nelson's candymakers were summoned to State Street to train the staff of the Field's candy kitchen in the intricacies of truffle making, and the candies became an instant Chicago favorite.

Today, Field's sells more than one million pounds of Frango chocolates each year. New flavors, from raspberry and caramel to dark mint and double chocolate, have been embraced by legions of Frango fans all over the world (though the original mint chocolate

is by far the number-one seller). Other Frango treats, including dessert toppings, chips, cookies, liqueurs, coffees, teas, and cocoa round out the line, and in Marshall Field's restaurants, Frango desserts, like Mint Chocolate Ice Cream Pie, Frango Chocolate Cheesecake, and Mint, Chocolate Chip Cookies remain hugely popular year after year.

Candyland in the Sky

For much of the twentieth century, the Field's candy kitchen on the thirteenth floor of the State Street store was the center of the Frango Mint universe. While most department stores smelled like perfume and cologne, at Field's, the aromas of melting chocolate and mint filled the air and permeated the walls, beckoning guests to see, smell, and indulge.

Candy kitchen confectioners would melt dark and milk chocolate in giant kettles and stir in a secret blend of flavorings and ingredients. The mixture was poured out to cool on marble slabs and cut into individual pieces, which were passed under a continuous shower of pure melted chocolate in an enrobing machine. Once cooled, the chocolates were nestled in paper cups and hand-packed in signature green boxes.

FRANGO FACTS

In 2003, a box containing more than a ton of Frango chocolates was included in Guinness World Records as the "Largest Box of Chocolates."

The Frango mint chocolate is the best-selling flavor, with double chocolate running a distant second.

Two hundred pounds of chocolate are melted to make each batch of Frango candy.

More than one million pounds of Frango chocolates are sold each year.

Year-round flavors include: mint, dark mint, sugar-free mint, double chocolate, caramel, toffee, raspberry, and the newest addition, dark chocolate.

Seasonal flavors have included everything from candy cane in winter to passion fruit in summer.

In 1999, to meet worldwide demand for Frango chocolates, the candy kitchen was moved to a larger, offsite facility, where Frango mints are still made using the same secret recipe. Technological advances have also enabled Field's to expand its assortment and develop new offerings, such as limited edition pink Frango mints created to raise funds for the Breast Cancer Research Foundation.

FRANGO HOT CHOCOLATE

Serves 4

If you can boil water (or in this case milk), you can make Marshall Field's ultra-decadent signature hot cocoa. It's nothing more than Frango chocolates and hot milk whipped in a blender, but you'll be amazed by its velvety richness. Try it with all your favorite Frango flavors. You can't go wrong.

Place the chocolates in a blender and pour in the hot milk. Place the lid on the blender, cover with a dishtowel, and blend on high speed for 15 seconds, until well blended and frothy. Divide among warm mugs and top with Frango chocolate shavings (made with a vegetable peeler). Serve at once.

9 Frango chocolates (any flavor, about 3 ounces), chopped, plus extra, for garnish

3 cups milk, heated

FRANGO RICE KRISPY TREATS

Makes 12 large bars

Field's famous Rice Krispy treats topped with a Frango chocolate layer have been written up in newspapers, featured on TV, discussed on the Internet, and enjoyed by thousands of guests, year after year. Here's the easy, no-bake recipe (pictured previous page).

Butter a 9 by 13-inch baking pan. Melt the butter in a large, heavy-bottomed saucepan over medium heat. Add the marshmallows and stir constantly for about 5 minutes, until completely melted and smooth. Watch carefully to avoid burning; decrease the heat if the mixture begins to brown.

Remove from the heat, add the cereal, and stir well to combine thoroughly. Scoop the mixture into the prepared pan. Butter your hands and firmly pat the mixture into the pan, making as even a layer as possible. Evenly sprinkle the chocolate chips over the top and use a rubber spatula to spread them out. (The heat from the mixture should soften the chips enough to spread them; if not, place the pan in a warm oven for 2 minutes to soften the chips.)

Allow the chocolate to harden at room temperature for 4 to 6 hours before cutting into 12 bars. Store at room temperature in an airtight container for up to 3 days.

6 tablespoons unsalted butter

18 ounces mini marshmallows

9 cups crispy rice cereal

12 ounces Frango Double Chocolate Baking Chips or chopped Frango double chocolate candies

MINT CHOCOLATE CHIP COOKIES

Makes 8 dozen cookies

The bakers at Field's do the Toll House cookie one better. Instead of the usual chips, these chewy cookies are studded with chunks of chopped Frango chocolates and pecans.

Position racks at the top and in the center of the oven and preheat to 350°F. Line 2 baking sheets with parchment paper (or use nonstick baking sheets).

Sift together the flour, baking soda, and salt into a bowl. Place the butter and shortening in a separate large bowl. Using an electric mixer on medium speed, cream the butter and shortening for about 1 minute, until blended. Add the sugars and beat for about 1 minute, until well mixed. Beat in the eggs, finely chopped chocolates, and vanilla. Add the flour mixture and, using a wooden spoon, stir until well blended. Stir in the coarsely chopped chocolate and pecans. Drop rounded teaspoons of the cookie dough 1 inch apart onto the prepared sheets.

Bake for about 10 minutes, until nearly firm but still soft to the touch in the center. Using a spatula, transfer the cookies to wire racks and allow to cool completely. Repeat with the remaining cookie dough, allowing the baking sheets to cool between batches. The cookies can be stored in an airtight container at room temperature for up to 5 days.

$2^1/_4$ cups all-purpose flour

1 teaspoon baking soda

$^1/_2$ teaspoon salt

$^1/_2$ cup unsalted butter, at room temperature

$^1/_2$ cup vegetable shortening, at room temperature

1 cup firmly packed light brown sugar

$^1/_2$ cup granulated sugar

2 eggs, at room temperature

5 Frango mint chocolates (about 2 ounces), very finely chopped

1 teaspoon pure vanilla extract

25 Frango mint chocolates (about 9 ounces), coarsely chopped

$^3/_4$ cup coarsely chopped pecans

FRANGO CHOCOLATE POTS DE CRÈME

Serves 6 | *These luscious individual chocolate custards are a fine choice for entertaining. You can make them a day or two ahead of time, and then take them out of the fridge at the start of the meal so they are at room temperature when it's time for dessert. If you want to experiment with other Frango chocolate flavors, mint, dark mint, and raspberry are particularly good.*

Preheat the oven to 300°F and place a rack in the center position. In a saucepan, bring the milk to a simmer over medium heat. Add the chopped chocolate and stir until melted. Remove from the heat and stir in the cream. Allow to cool slightly.

In a bowl, whisk together the egg yolks and sugar until well combined but not foamy. Slowly pour the chocolate mixture into the egg yolk mixture, stirring constantly. Strain through a fine-mesh sieve and let rest at room temperature for 10 minutes.

Divide the mixture among six 3/4-cup ramekins or soufflé dishes. Set the ramekins in a baking dish and place the dish in the oven. Pour hot water into the baking dish to reach halfway up the sides of the ramekins. Cover the pan with aluminum foil and bake for 45 minutes to 1 hour, until just set at the edges but still soft in the center. Do not over bake.

Remove from the oven and allow to cool. Serve warm or at room temperature, or cover and refrigerate for up to 2 days and serve chilled. Top with a dollop of whipped cream and a pinch of Frango chocolate shavings (made with a vegetable peeler) and serve.

1 cup whole milk

16 Frango chocolates (any flavor, about 6 ounces), chopped, plus extra for garnish

1 1/2 cups heavy cream

6 egg yolks

1/3 cup granulated sugar

Whipped cream, for serving

FLOURLESS FRANGO DOUBLE CHOCOLATE CAKES

Serves 6

Do you love those intense warm chocolate cakes so many restaurants are serving these days? This easy home version is made with just three ingredients. Instead of ramekins, you can use mini muffin tins (skip the foil and bake for 6 to 8 minutes, until puffed) or an 8-inch cake pan (bake as directed, allow to cool, and invert onto a plate to unmold). Whichever way you go, watch carefully and err on the side of underbaking so the center is a bit runny. For best effect, serve warm with vanilla bean ice cream and fresh raspberries.

Preheat the oven to 425°F. Bring a pot of water to a simmer. Combine the chocolate chips and butter in a stainless steel bowl and place over, but not touching, the simmering water. Heat, stirring often, for 5 to 7 minutes, until melted and smooth. Remove the bowl from the heat.

Place the eggs in a separate stainless steel bowl. Place over, but not touching, the simmering water and heat, stirring constantly, until just warm to the touch. Remove the bowl from the heat. Using an electric mixer on high speed, whip the eggs until light and foamy. Fold the eggs into the chocolate mixture and combine completely.

Generously grease six 8-ounce ramekins or heat-proof cups with nonstick spray or butter. Divide the chocolate mixture equally among the ramekins.

Set the ramekins on a baking sheet and bake for 5 minutes, then cover with aluminum foil and bake for 15 minutes. Remove from the oven and serve immediately or allow to cool to room temperature before serving.

1 pound Frango Double Chocolate Baking Chips

1 cup unsalted butter

6 large eggs

TRIPLE-TREAT CHOCOLATE LAYER CAKE

Serves 10 to 12 | *Go ahead. Give this luscious layer cake with a fluffy Frango frosting a try. Even non-bakers find it remarkably foolproof. You can wrap the layers tightly in plastic wrap and foil and freeze them for up to a month, then thaw, assemble, and ice when that birthday or special occasion rolls around.*

TO PREPARE THE CAKE, position racks in the center and at the top of the oven and preheat to 350°F. Lightly butter the bottom and sides of three 9-inch round cake pans. Line the bottom of the pans with circles of parchment paper. Dust the pans with flour and tap out the excess.

In a small bowl, cover the chopped chocolates and unsweetened chocolate with the boiling water and let stand for 1 minute. Whisk the mixture until smooth and allow to cool to room temperature.

In a bowl, sift together the flour, cocoa, baking soda, and salt. Place the butter in a separate large bowl. Using an electric mixer on medium-high speed, beat the butter for about 1 minute, until creamy. Gradually add the sugar and beat for about 2 minutes, until light and fluffy. One at a time, add the eggs, beating well after each addition. Beat in the chocolate mixture and vanilla. One-third at a time, alternately add the flour mixture and the buttermilk, beating well after each addition and scraping the sides of the bowl with a rubber spatula as necessary. Divide the batter equally among the prepared pans and smooth the tops.

Bake for 15 minutes, then switch the positions of the cakes from front to back and top to bottom. Continue baking for 15 to 20 minutes, until the cakes spring back when lightly touched in the center and a toothpick inserted in the center comes out clean. Transfer the cakes in the pans to wire racks and allow to cool for 10 minutes. Invert the cakes onto the racks, carefully peel off the paper, and allow to cool completely.

continued

CAKE

6 Frango mint dark chocolates (about 2 ounces), finely chopped

2 ounces unsweetened chocolate, finely chopped

1/2 cup boiling water

2 1/2 cups cake flour

1/4 cup unsweetened cocoa powder (preferably not Dutch process)

1 teaspoon baking soda

1/2 teaspoon salt

1 cup unsalted butter, at room temperature

2 cups sugar

4 eggs, at room temperature

3/4 teaspoon pure vanilla extract

1 cup buttermilk, at room temperature

FROSTING

12 Frango mint dark chocolates (about 4 ounces), finely chopped

2 ounces unsweetened chocolate, finely chopped

2 1/4 cups unsalted butter, at room temperature

1 cup plus 2 tablespoons confectioners' sugar, sifted

15 Frango mint dark chocolates (about 5 1/2 ounces), finely chopped, for garnish

TO PREPARE THE FROSTING, heat a pot of water until it is steaming but not simmering. Combine the chopped chocolates and unsweetened chocolate in a stainless steel bowl and place over, but not touching, the hot water. Heat, stirring often, for 5 to 7 minutes, until smooth. Remove the bowl from the heat and let stand until cool but still liquid.

Place the butter in a large bowl. Using an electric mixer on medium-high speed, beat the butter for about 1 minute, until creamy. Decrease the speed to low and gradually add the confectioners' sugar. Increase the speed to medium-high and beat for about 2 minutes, until light and fluffy. Add the chocolate mixture and beat, scraping the sides of the bowl with a rubber spatula, until smooth.

Place one cake layer upside down on a serving platter. Using a cake spatula, spread about 1 cup of the frosting evenly over the top. Top with a second cake layer, also upside down, and spread with 1 cup of the frosting. Place the third cake layer upside down on the top. Evenly frost the top and sides of the entire cake with the remaining frosting. Sprinkle the top of the cake with the additional chopped Frango chocolates. The cake can be covered and kept at room temperature for up to 2 days.

MINT CHOCOLATE ICE CREAM PIE

Serves 6 to 8

If you grew up in Chicago, this time-honored Walnut Room treat may well have been your first restaurant dessert. It's a classic graham cracker crust with a homemade ice cream filling that's frozen soft and rushed from the kitchen to arrive at the table just as it's beginning to melt. If you don't have time to make this from scratch, you can create a reasonable facsimile using softened, store-bought, chocolate ice cream with chopped Frango mint chocolates stirred in.

TO PREPARE THE CRUST, position a rack in the center of the oven and preheat to 350°F. Butter a 9-inch pie pan. Combine the cracker crumbs, butter, and sugar in a food processor and process until well blended. Transfer to the prepared pie pan and press the mixture evenly and firmly into the bottom and sides of the pan. Bake for about 8 minutes, until the crust is beginning to brown. Transfer to a wire rack and allow to cool completely in the pan.

TO PREPARE THE FILLING, in a heavy-bottomed saucepan, combine the sugar, cornstarch, and salt. Add $1/4$ cup of the milk and whisk until the cornstarch is dissolved. Add the chocolates and the remaining $3/4$ cup milk and place over medium-low heat. Cook, stirring constantly, for about 4 minutes, until the mixture comes to a boil. Remove the pan from the heat.

In a small bowl, whisk the egg until lightly beaten. Gradually add about $1/4$ cup of the hot chocolate mixture to the egg, whisking constantly until blended. Whisk the chocolate and egg mixture back into the saucepan and place over low heat. Cook, stirring constantly, for about 1 minute, until slightly thickened. Do not let the mixture come near a boil or the eggs will scramble. Transfer the custard to a bowl and allow to cool completely, stirring occasionally. Stir in the cream and vanilla. Refrigerate for about 2 hours, until well chilled.

continued

CRUST

$1^1/2$ cups graham cracker crumbs (about 18 crackers)

6 tablespoons unsalted butter, melted

$1/4$ cup sugar

FILLING

$1/2$ cup sugar

$1^1/2$ teaspoons cornstarch

$1/8$ teaspoon salt

1 cup milk

8 Frango mint chocolates (about 3 ounces), finely chopped

1 egg, at room temperature

1 cup heavy whipping cream

$1/2$ teaspoon pure vanilla extract

TOPPING

$1/2$ cup sugar

$1/2$ cup toasted, skinned, and coarsely chopped hazelnuts (see note)

Whipped cream, for garnish

Freeze the custard in an ice cream maker according to the manufacturer's instructions, until frozen but soft and spreadable. Transfer the ice cream to the crust and smooth the top with a spatula. Cover tightly with plastic wrap and freeze for at least 4 hours or overnight, until very firm.

TO PREPARE THE TOPPING, butter a baking sheet. Combine the sugar and hazelnuts in a heavy-bottomed, small saucepan over medium heat. Cook, stirring constantly, for about 5 minutes, until the sugar starts to dissolve. Decrease the heat to low and continue stirring for about 5 minutes, until the hazelnuts are well coated and the sugar is caramelized (some of the sugar may remain unmelted). Pour the caramelized hazelnuts onto the prepared baking sheet. Transfer the baking sheet to a wire rack and allow to cool completely.

Using your hands, break the hazelnut praline into small pieces and transfer to a food processor. Pulse until finely chopped.

Sprinkle the top of the pie with the hazelnut praline, pressing it in gently to adhere. Garnish with whipped cream and serve immediately. The pie can be stored in the freezer for up to 1 week, covered tightly in plastic wrap and then aluminum foil.

TOASTING AND SKINNING HAZELNUTS: Preheat the oven to 350°F. Line a baking sheet with aluminum foil and spread the hazelnuts on the baking sheet in a single layer. Bake, shaking the pan once or twice, for 10 minutes, until the nuts are lightly browned and fragrant. Wrap the nuts in a clean dishtowel and allow to cool for 10 minutes. Rub the nuts in the towel to remove their papery skins.

FRANGO CHOCOLATE CHEESECAKE

Serves 8

This is Field's cheesecake for chocolate lovers: mint chocolate cheesecake, a Frango sour cream topping, and a semisweet chocolate glaze—all layered onto a chocolate cookie crust. It's not hard to make, but you do need to allow plenty of time for the baking, cooling, topping, and glazing steps.

Place a rack in the center of the oven and preheat to 350°F.

TO PREPARE THE CRUST, combine the cookie crumbs, butter, and sugar in a food processor and process until well blended. Transfer to an ungreased 8-inch-round, 2-inch-deep springform pan and press evenly and firmly into the bottom of the pan.

TO PREPARE THE FILLING, heat a pot of water until it is steaming but not simmering. Place the chocolates in a stainless steel bowl and place over, but not touching, the hot water. Heat, stirring often, for 5 to 7 minutes, until melted and smooth. Remove the chocolate from the heat and allow to cool until tepid.

Place the cream cheese in a large bowl. Using an electric mixer on medium speed, beat the cream cheese until smooth. Add the sugar and blend well. Add the eggs one at a time, blending well after each addition, stopping occasionally to scrape down the sides of the bowl and the beaters. Add the chocolate, cream, and vanilla and beat until well mixed. Pour into the crust.

Bake for about 35 minutes, until the sides of the cake rise and the top jiggles slightly when shaken. (The cake will appear underbaked, but will firm upon chilling.) Run a sharp knife around the inside of the pan to release the cake from the sides. Transfer the cake to a wire rack and allow to cool completely in the pan.

continued

CRUST

1 cup chocolate wafer cookie crumbs (about 20 cookies)

4 tablespoons unsalted butter, melted

1 tablespoon plus 2 teaspoons sugar

FILLING

15 Frango mint chocolates (about 5 1/2 ounces), coarsely chopped

3 (8-ounce) packages cream cheese, at room temperature

1 cup sugar

2 eggs, at room temperature

1/3 cup heavy whipping cream

1/2 teaspoon pure vanilla extract

TO PREPARE THE TOPPING, heat a pot of water until it is steaming but not simmering. Combine the gelatin and water in a stainless steel bowl until the gelatin is softened. Place the bowl over, but not touching, the hot water and stir for about 3 minutes, until the gelatin is dissolved. Add the chocolates and stir for 2 to 3 minutes, until melted. Remove the chocolate mixture from the heat and allow to cool until tepid. Whisk the sour cream into the chocolate mixture until blended. Evenly spread the topping on top of the cheesecake and refrigerate for 4 hours, until completely chilled.

TO PREPARE THE GLAZE, bring the cream to a boil in a small saucepan over medium-high heat. Remove from the heat, add the chocolate, and stir until melted. Add the butter and whisk until melted. Let rest at room temperature for 30 minutes, until cooled and thickened. With the sides of the pan still in place, pour the glaze evenly over the cheesecake and refrigerate for about 30 minutes, until set. The cake can be covered and refrigerated for up to 2 days.

To serve, slice the cake and garnish each slice with a dollop of whipped cream, a few Little O's candies, and a mint sprig.

TOPPING

$1/4$ teaspoon unflavored gelatin

1 tablespoon cold water

3 Frango mint chocolates
   (about 1 ounce), finely chopped

$1/2$ cup sour cream, at room temperature

GLAZE

$3/4$ cup heavy whipping cream

3 ounces semisweet chocolate, finely
   chopped

2 tablespoons unsalted butter

Whipped cream, for garnish

Frango Mint Little O's candies, for
   garnish

Mint sprigs, for garnish

RASPBERRY DELIGHT TART

Serves 6 to 8

When sweet red raspberries appear at your local farmers' market, celebrate by making this elegantly simple tart with a deep dark Frango raspberry chocolate filling and wall-to-wall berries on top.

TO PREPARE THE CRUST, in a bowl, stir together the flour, sugar, and salt. Using a pastry blender or 2 knives, cut the butter into the dry ingredients until the mixture resembles coarse meal.

In a small bowl, stir together the egg yolk and ice water. Add to the flour mixture and stir just until the dough comes together. (If the dough seems too dry, sprinkle in additional ice water, 1 teaspoon at a time, until moist enough to hold together.) Form the dough into a flat disk, cover tightly with plastic wrap, and refrigerate for about 1 hour, until well chilled.

Lightly flour a work surface. Using a floured rolling pin, roll the dough out into an 11-inch circle. Gently transfer the dough to a 9-inch tart pan. Fold over the edges of the dough to make a double layer and press against the sides of the pan, making sure there are no air pockets. Trim the excess dough by pressing it against the fluted edge. Prick the bottom of the dough with a fork. Cover loosely with plastic wrap. Freeze for 30 minutes.

Position a rack in the bottom third of the oven and preheat to 400°F. Line the crust with a piece of aluminum foil and fill it with pie weights or dried beans. Bake for 10 minutes, remove the weights and foil, and continue to bake for about 10 minutes, until uniformly golden. Transfer to a wire rack and allow to cool completely in the pan.

TO PREPARE THE FILLING, melt the butter over low heat in a small saucepan. Remove the pan from the heat. Add the chocolates and let stand for 1 minute. Whisk until smooth. Add the cream and whisk until well combined. Pour the filling into the pie shell. Standing them upright, arrange the raspberries in concentric circles to cover the filling.

Cover with plastic wrap. Refrigerate for at least 4 hours or overnight, until the filling is firm. Sift confectioners' sugar over the top before serving. The tart can be covered and stored in the refrigerator for 1 day.

CRUST

1 cup all-purpose flour

2 tablespoons sugar

$1/8$ teaspoon salt

5 tablespoons plus 1 teaspoon cold unsalted butter, cut into $1/2$-inch pieces

1 egg yolk, chilled

2 teaspoons ice water

FILLING

$1/2$ cup unsalted butter

18 Frango raspberry chocolates (about $6^{1}/2$ ounces), finely chopped

$1/3$ cup heavy whipping cream, at room temperature

$1^{1}/2$ cups fresh raspberries

Confectioners' sugar, for garnish

HOLIDAY

Holiday Heaven

Ask any fan of Field's about their childhood memories of the store and they'll say one word: Christmas.

Back in 1907, a Field's busboy was dispatched to find a Christmas tree to spruce up the Walnut Room. That little tree soon grew into a grand Chicago tradition. For nearly a century of Christmases, the Walnut Room's Great Tree has filled the restaurant's two-story atrium. Each fall until the 1960s (when fire codes required the use of an artificial tree), members of Field's special Tree Design Bureau would scope out a suitably symmetrical, seventy-foot balsam fir in the forests along Lake Superior. The top forty-five feet would be felled, bundled, and hauled through the snow by sled to a waiting railway flatcar bound for Chicago.

Once it arrived at State Street, the tree would be carefully threaded through the store's front entrance (the revolving doors had to be removed) and hoisted up seven stories through the light well to its home for the holidays—a platform over the fountain in the Walnut Room.

Mr. and Mrs. Joseph Clark haven't missed a Walnut Room Christmas in 57 years.

Today's Great Tree is still forty-five feet tall—and it's still one of the most beloved Christmas trees in the world. From November until the first week of January, some twenty-five thousand people come to admire it every day. Its theme and décor change annually, with a single tree requiring up to three years of planning. After all, it takes twelve hundred ornaments and fifteen thousand lights to trim a tree this size. Recently, designers from such renowned companies as Swarovski and Waterford have created breathtaking trees adorned from trunk to tip in sparkling crystal.

Find yourself a table beside the Great Tree and you'll see generations of happy guests enjoying an annual family tradition. The kids are eating Snowman Sundaes and munching on Santa Bear Cookies. Their parents and grandparents are savoring their meal, and resting their tired feet, perhaps recalling their own childhood memories—the magical window displays, the fourth-floor Land of Toys, and the visits to Santa and his helper, a Marshall Field's creation known as Uncle Mistletoe. And here and there, you'll see a few beaming great-grandparents, who can still remember the wonder they felt seventy, eighty, maybe even ninety years ago, when they first stared up at those shimmering branches and their hearts were filled with magic and joy.

SANTA BEAR COOKIES

Makes 10 large cookies

Another beloved Marshall Field's tradition. Each year, the company creates a collectible teddy bear dressed in a Santa outfit and commissions a limited-edition mug and a decorated cookie to match. When kids order hot cider or cocoa at the Walnut Room, they get to keep the mug. With this recipe, you can start your own Santa Bear tradition at home.

Combine the granulated sugar, butter, and shortening in a bowl or a stand mixer fitted with the paddle attachment. Using medium speed, cream until fluffy. Add the egg, vanilla, and baking powder and mix well. Decrease the speed to low, add the flour, and mix until the dough starts to come together. Shape the dough into a large flat disk, kneading briefly if necessary to bring it completely together. Cover with plastic wrap and refrigerate for 1 to 2 hours.

Preheat the oven to 350°F. Butter a baking sheet. On a lightly floured surface, roll the dough out to $1/4$ inch thick. Using 6-inch-tall bear-shaped cookie cutters, cut the dough into shapes. Transfer to the prepared baking sheet and chill for 15 to 30 minutes. Bake for 20 to 25 minutes, until light golden. Allow to cool completely on the baking sheet.

TO PREPARE THE ICING, combine the confectioners' sugar, 6 tablespoons of the milk, and the vanilla in a bowl and stir until smooth. If the icing is too thick to spread, add the remaining 3 tablespoons milk a little at a time, until it is smooth and pourable, but thick enough to coat. Measure $1/4$ cup of the icing into each of 3 small bowls (you will still have some white icing left in the mixing bowl). Add drops of coloring to each of the small bowls to make red, green, and yellow icing.

Heat a saucepan of water to a low simmer. Put the chocolate in a stainless steel bowl and place over, but not touching, the hot water. Heat, stirring often, for 5 to 7 minutes, until melted and smooth.

continued

$3/4$ cup granulated sugar

$3/4$ cup unsalted butter, at room temperature

$2/3$ cup vegetable shortening

1 egg

$1/4$ teaspoon pure vanilla extract

$1/2$ teaspoon baking powder

$3 1/2$ cups all-purpose flour

ICING

6 cups confectioners' sugar

6 to 9 tablespoons milk

$3/4$ teaspoon pure vanilla extract

Red, green, and yellow food coloring

3 ounces semisweet chocolate

Transfer the colored icings to squeeze bottles or parchment-paper cones. Transfer the warm chocolate into a bottle or cone just before you are ready to use it. If using cones, flatten them, fold the large end over a few times to enclose the icing or chocolate, and snip off the tip of the cone. Set a wire rack over a piece of wax or parchment paper. Place the cookies on the rack and divide the white icing among them, spreading it out evenly with a metal icing spatula. Let the white icing set for a few minutes, then use the chocolate and colored icings to decorate the bears. Allow to set for 1 hour before serving. The cookies can be stored in an airtight container for up to 3 days.

SNOWMAN

Serves 4

Meet the little snowman that could. He may be nothing more than a cleverly decorated scoop of ice cream, but this cheery character has been making children smile at the Walnut Room for more than fifty holiday seasons. During November and December at State Street, a designated marshmallow artist hand-paints more than two thousand snowman faces a week.

Make the snowmen's heads by painting a face on each marshmallow, using a toothpick dipped in the food coloring.

Place 1 scoop of ice cream in each of 4 chilled dessert dishes. Arrange 3 raisins in a line down the center of each scoop to resemble buttons. Top each scoop with one of the marshmallow heads. Place half a cherry on top of each marshmallow to make hats. Stick 2 licorice twists into each scoop of ice cream for arms. Serve at once.

4 marshmallows

Red food coloring, watered down

4 scoops vanilla ice cream

12 raisins, chocolate chips, or dried cranberries

2 maraschino cherries, halved

4 red licorice twists, halved, or 8 candy canes or cookie sticks

PLUM PUDDING

Serves 10 to 12

Field's Culinary Council Chef Gale Gand came up with this moist, rich version of the classic English Christmas treat. To prepare the vegetable shortening, she recommends spreading it in a thin layer on a piece of foil and scoring cross-hatch marks in it with a knife. Once frozen, the shortening will pop off the foil in pieces. You can also freeze sticks of shortening and grate them on the large holes of a box grater.

Grease an 8-cup metal or ceramic pudding mold with butter and then dust with sugar. Sift together the flour, salt, baking soda, nutmeg, cinnamon, cloves, and allspice into a bowl. Add the breadcrumbs, shortening, dried plum purée, brown sugar, dried plums, lemon peel, molasses, and egg yolks and mix well. In a separate bowl, whip the egg whites until stiff. Fold the egg whites into the batter. Pour the batter into the prepared mold. Cover the mold tightly with its lid or with 2 layers of aluminum foil.

Set a steaming rack inside a large pot, or use a plate on top of crumpled aluminum foil. (The rack or plate will suspend the mold above the water.) Pour 2 inches of water into the pot and bring to a boil over high heat. Set the covered pudding mold on the rack. Cover the pot, decrease the heat to medium-low, and steam for $1^1/_2$ to 2 hours, depending on the size of your mold, until puffed and set. Be sure to maintain the water level throughout the steaming process.

TO PREPARE THE SAUCE, in a bowl, cream the butter using an electric mixer until pale in color. Add the sugar and mix well. Add the rum and vanilla and mix well. Taste and adjust the flavoring as necessary.

Serve the pudding warm with a dollop of the hard sauce spooned on top. Or you can soak the pudding with 1 ounce of brandy and store it in the refrigerator to serve later. Add 1 ounce of brandy each week for up to 6 months.

DRIED PLUM PURÉE: Canned dried plum purée (also called prune purée) can be purchased in specialty foods stores. To make your own, combine 8 ounces ($8^1/_3$ cups) pitted dried plums and 6 tablespoons water in the bowl of a food processor. Purée until a smooth paste is formed. Makes 1 cup. Can be refrigerated, covered, for up to 1 month.

1 cup all-purpose flour

$^1/_2$ teaspoon salt

$^1/_2$ teaspoon baking soda

$^1/_2$ teaspoon ground nutmeg

$^1/_2$ teaspoon ground cinnamon

$^1/_2$ teaspoon ground cloves

$^1/_2$ teaspoon ground allspice

1 cup soft breadcrumbs

1 cup vegetable shortening, frozen and finely chopped or grated

1 cup dried plum (prune) purée (see note)

$^1/_2$ cup packed brown sugar

1 cup chopped dried plums (prunes)

$^1/_4$ cup finely chopped candied lemon peel

$^1/_4$ cup molasses

3 eggs, separated

HARD SAUCE

4 tablespoons unsalted butter

1 cup confectioners' sugar

1 tablespoon dark rum

$^1/_2$ teaspoon pure vanilla extract

FRESH TAKES

From the Field's Culinary Council

FIELD'S CULINARY COUNCIL

Meet the Field's Culinary Council—twelve of America's favorite chefs. They are restaurant owners, authors, TV stars, teachers, and tastemakers. They bring a whole world of cooking styles and traditions to Field's— Chinese, Japanese, Mexican, Mediterranean, Ethiopian, Swedish, and American. But diversity is only part of what makes this group so special. What's even more striking is what they have in common: a shared enthusiasm for simple unpretentious excellence; honesty in the kitchen and on the plate; bright, true flavors; and, most of all, fun. These folks live large.

For this book, each of them was given the same challenge: Come up with a "fresh take" on Field's culinary icon, *Mrs. Hering's Famous Chicken Potpie* (page 65) and one other favorite Field's recipe. You'll find this symbol ▯ next to these recipes.

In addition, each chef contributed two treasured family recipes of their own—easy dishes that are perfect for a weeknight dinner or a casual meal with friends. If there's a single message behind all of these fresh takes, it's this: eat well, have fun, and live large.

LEFT TO RIGHT: Andrea Robinson, Rick Bayless, Tyler Florence, Ming Tsai, Marcus Samuelsson, Tim Scott, Gale Gand, Todd English, Nancy Silverton, Tom Douglas, Elizabeth Brown, Takashi Yagihashi.

Rick Bayless is a chef on a quest. Through his restaurants, books, and television series, he's constantly exploring new ways to bring the beauty and complexity of Mexican cooking to the American table. Rick learned to crawl, walk, wash dishes, and eventually cook at his family's Oklahoma City barbecue restaurant, the Hickory House. He fell in love with Mexico as a teenager, and studied Spanish and Latin American culture in college. A few years later, his passions all came together when he fired up his VW van and took off with his wife, Deann, on a six-year eating odyssey through every region of Mexico: tasting, studying, and compiling notes for what would become his definitive Mexican cookbook, *Authentic Mexican*, the first of many successful books. Rick is chef-owner of two beloved Chicago restaurants, Frontera Grill and Topolobampo, and host of the popular public television series, *Mexico One Plate at a Time*.

POBLANO POTPIE

Serves 4

Rick wants the world to know that enjoying the exciting flavors of Mexico at home doesn't have to mean mastering all kinds of exotic Latin ingredients. This recipe has just two—poblano peppers and cilantro—and they're both sold in most supermarkets. That's all it takes to turn a classic American chicken 'n' biscuits potpie into a one-pan supper that can satisfy those "I want something Mexican" cravings any night of the week.

Rick's fresh take on Mrs. Hering's Potpie, page 65

Position a rack in the top third of the oven and preheat to 425°F.

TO PREPARE THE BISCUITS, whisk the milk and egg together in a small bowl. Combine the flour, baking powder, sugar, and salt in a food processor and pulse four times to mix. Add the butter and pulse eight times. With the motor running, slowly pour the milk-egg mixture through the feed tube and mix for about 4 seconds, until the dough comes together into a sticky-looking mass; do not overmix. Pulse as necessary until all the flour is moistened. Turn the dough out onto a heavily floured work surface. Dust the dough with flour. Knead gently 5 times (use a little more flour if necessary to prevent sticking). Form the dough into a 9-inch round. Using a biscuit cutter or an upside down glass, cut into four 2- to 3-inch biscuits.

TO PREPARE THE FILLING, roast the peppers over an open flame or 4 inches below a broiler until blistered and blackened all over. Place in a bowl, cover with a kitchen towel, and allow to cool for about 20 minutes. Rub the blackened skin off the peppers and pull out the stems and seed-pods. Rinse the flesh to remove any remaining bits of skin and seeds. Cut into 1/4-inch pieces.

BISCUITS

1/2 cup milk

1 egg

1 1/2 cups all-purpose flour, plus extra for kneading

2 1/2 teaspoons baking powder

1 teaspoon sugar

1/2 teaspoon salt

6 tablespoons cold unsalted butter, cut into 12 pieces

FILLING

2 large poblano peppers

2 tablespoons unsalted butter or vegetable oil

1 small onion, chopped in 1/4-inch dice

1/4 cup all-purpose flour

2 1/4 cups milk

1 pound boneless skinless chicken thighs, cut into 1-inch squares (about 2 1/2 cups)

Melt the butter or heat the oil in a medium saucepan over medium heat. Add the peppers and onion and cook, stirring frequently, for about 6 minutes, until they begin to brown. Add the flour and stir thoroughly. Add half of the milk and whisk constantly until the mixture thickens. Add the remaining milk and whisk until the mixture boils. Add the chicken, carrots, salt, pepper, and thyme and stir well. Decrease the heat to medium-low and simmer for 10 minutes. Taste and add salt if necessary. Add the peas and cilantro and stir well. Scoop the mixture into an 8 by 8-inch baking dish, spreading it out evenly. Lay the biscuits on top in a single layer.

Set the baking dish on a baking sheet. Bake for 25 minutes, until the biscuits are browned. Serve while still hot.

2 carrots, cut into small pieces

1 teaspoon salt

$1/2$ teaspoon freshly ground black pepper

1 teaspoon fresh thyme leaves, or $1/4$ teaspoon dried thyme

1 cup frozen peas

$1/2$ cup cilantro, chopped

"One way to speed up everyday cooking: get the small stuff—small potatoes, baby green beans and carrots, or precut vegetables like mushrooms and broccoli florets. You'll save prep time, and small ingredients cook faster too."

GRILLED CHICKEN SALAD

with Rustic Guacamole, Romaine, and Aged Mexican Cheese

Serves 4

"Here's a salad to entice folks out of the 'grilled chicken Caesar' rut," says Rick. "True, it starts with grilled chicken, but chicken that's redolent of roasted garlic, green chile, cilantro, and lime, chicken that dances the cumbia with guacamole, crisp romaine, and nutty aged cheese. The flavors are so captivating that you can even get away without firing up the grill—this is a perfect place to put a stovetop grill pan to work."

TO PREPARE THE DRESSSING, heat the oil in a small skillet over medium heat. Add the garlic and chiles, and cook, stirring frequently, until the garlic is soft and lightly browned, usually 1 to 2 minutes. Pour the oil, garlic, and chiles into a blender or food processor. Add the lime juice, cilantro, salt, and pepper. Process until smooth.

Place the chicken breasts in a shallow, nonreactive pan. Pour one-third of the garlic mixture over the chicken and spread it evenly over all sides.

Heat a grill pan over medium heat or preheat a gas grill to medium-high (or start a charcoal fire and let it burn until the coals are medium hot and covered with white ash). Lightly brush or spray the onion slices with oil; sprinkle with salt. Lay the chicken and onion onto the grill pan or grill rack. Cook until the chicken is just cooked through and the onion is well browned, 3 to 4 minutes on each side. Chop the onion into small pieces and scoop into a bowl.

Pit and peel the avocados, scooping the flesh into the bowl with the onion. Add another one-third of the garlic mixture, then coarsely mash everything together with an old-fashioned potato masher, large fork, or the back of a spoon. Taste and season with salt, usually about $^1/_2$ teaspoon.

Place the sliced romaine in a large bowl. Drizzle on the remaining one-third of the garlic mixture and toss to combine. Divide between 4 dinner plates. Scoop a portion of the guacamole into the center of each plate. Cut each chicken breast into cubes and arrange over the guacamole. Sprinkle each plate with the queso añejo and you're ready to serve.

DRESSING

$^1/_2$ cup vegetable or olive oil, plus a little more for the onion

4 cloves garlic, halved

Fresh hot green chiles to taste (such as 2 serranos or 1 large jalapeño), stemmed and halved

$^1/_2$ cup freshly squeezed lime juice

$^3/_4$ cup (loosely packed) roughly chopped cilantro

1 scant teaspoon salt

$^1/_4$ teaspoon freshly ground black pepper

4 medium boneless skinless chicken breast halves (about $1^1/_4$ pounds total)

1 white onion, cut into $^1/_2$-inch slices

Salt

2 ripe avocados

Romaine hearts, sliced crosswise $^1/_2$ inch thick (about 8 cups)

About $^1/_3$ cup grated queso añejo, or other garnishing cheese like Romano or Parmesan

SKIRT STEAK SALAD
with "Wilted" Greens, Tomato, Avocado, and Lime

Serves 4

Served with a thick slice of seven-grain bread from the neighborhood bakery, this hearty salad is Rick's idea of one incredibly satisfying dinner. "I love the extra-beefy flavor of skirt steak, the rustic chew of the frisée (salad spinach is also good), and the savory pleasure of the warm, chipotle-infused dressing," he says. "And the creamy avocado and ripe tomato don't hurt either." Rick recommends using the thicker, more tender outer skirt steak. It should already be trimmed of the exterior white membrane and surface fat when you buy it.

Rick's fresh take on Flagship Sirloin Steak Salad, page 44

Scoop the frisée into a large bowl. Strew the chopped tomatoes and avocado over the top.

Set a very large (12-inch) heavy skillet over medium-high heat and add 2 tablespoons of the oil. Sprinkle both sides of the steak with salt and pepper. Lay it in the hot oil and cook until it's about medium-rare, 1 to 1¹⁄₂ minutes on each side. Transfer to a cooking rack set over a plate— this keeps the juices in the meat, rather than running out onto the plate.

Turn the heat under the skillet to low. Add the garlic and stir for a few seconds until very aromatic. Then pour in the broth (or water) and stir to release any browned bits on the bottom of the skillet (the liquid will quickly come to a boil). Turn off the heat and add the chile, lime juice, and remaining 4 tablespoons of the oil. Season with salt (usually ¹⁄₂ teaspoon) and pepper (about ¹⁄₄ teaspoon is right for me).

Cut the steak into roughly 3-inch lengths, then cut each piece across the grain into ¹⁄₄-inch strips. Add to the bowl with the frisée. Pour the warm dressing over the frisée and toss to coat thoroughly—the greens will wilt slightly. Divide between dinner plates or large salad bowls. Sprinkle with the grated cheese and serve right away.

1 medium-large (8-ounce) head frisée/curly endive, trimmed and cut into 2-inch sections (about 8 cups), or 8 cups salad spinach, long stems removed

2 medium-large ripe tomatoes, cored and cut into ¹⁄₂-inch cubes

2 medium avocados, peeled, pitted, and cut into ¹⁄₂-inch cubes

6 tablespoons vegetable or olive oil

1 pound skirt steak, trimmed of membrane and fat

Salt and freshly ground black pepper

2 to 3 cloves garlic, finely chopped or crushed through a garlic press

¹⁄₄ cup beef broth or water

1 chipotle chile en adobo, stemmed, seeds scraped out, and finely chopped

¹⁄₄ cup freshly squeezed lime juice

About ¹⁄₃ cup grated queso añejo or other dry grating cheese, such as Romano or Parmesan

PEACH COBBLER

Serves 10

Back in the sixties, Rick's red-haired Grandma Gladys would pile all the grandkids into her pointy-tailed Cadillac and head south from Oklahoma City toward Ardmore to pick peaches. ("Two hours, one stop at Stuckey's," he recalls.) Back at Grandma's, the peaches got turned into jam and butters, pickled, and canned in light syrup. "All year long, peaches would anchor our family meals," says Rick. Nowadays, his daughter, Lanie, carries on the tradition with this family recipe—a classic fresh peach cobbler with a golden lattice crust that, she says, "always gets tons of compliments."

TO PREPARE THE DOUGH, combine the flour, baking powder, salt, butter, and cream cheese in a food processor. Pulse 6 or 7 times until the mixture looks like coarse crumbs. Evenly drizzle in the vinegar and water. Pulse about 6 times until the mixture begins to clump together—it won't form a ball. Turn the dough out onto a large sheet of plastic wrap. Press the pieces of dough together, gather the plastic wrap over the top, then flatten into a 10 by 10-inch square. Refrigerate for 1 hour.

TO PREPARE THE FILLING, in a large bowl, mix together the peaches, sugar, cornstarch, nutmeg, lemon juice, and salt.

Position a rack in the middle of the oven and preheat to 400°F. Unwrap the dough and cut off about one-third of it. Rewrap and refrigerate this smaller piece. Evenly flour a work surface and the remaining two-thirds of the dough. Roll the dough out into a 14 by 18-inch rectangle. Drape into a 9 by 13-inch glass baking dish, easing the dough all the way into the corners and allowing a little to hang over the top rim of the dish. (If your kitchen is hot, refrigerate the dough-lined baking dish.)

Reflour the work surface and evenly flour the smaller piece of dough. Roll out into a 10 by 14-inch rectangle. Cut the dough lengthwise into ten 1-inch strips.

continued

DOUGH

2 2/3 cups all-purpose flour

1/4 teaspoon baking powder

1 teaspoon salt

1 cup cold unsalted butter

2 (3-ounce) packages cream cheese, chilled, cut into small pieces

1 tablespoon apple cider vinegar

3 tablespoons cold water

FILLING

5 pounds ripe peaches, peeled and cut into 1/2-inch pieces (about 6 cups)

1 to 1 1/4 cups sugar, plus a little extra for sprinkling

5 tablespoons cornstarch

1/2 heaping teaspoon grated nutmeg

1 1/2 tablespoons freshly squeezed lemon or lime juice

1/2 teaspoon salt

A little milk, for brushing over crust

2 tablespoons unsalted butter, cut into small pieces

Brush the top edge of the overhanging dough with a light coating of milk—just enough to make it sticky. Pour the fruit mixture into the pan. Dot the butter pieces over the filling. Lay 4 strips of the dough at even intervals lengthwise over the fruit. Lay the remaining 6 strips of dough at even intervals crosswise over the fruit, creating a lattice. Use a fork to seal the strips to the moistened edges. Trim off any overhanging dough. Brush the lattice with milk and sprinkle with a little sugar.

Bake the cobbler for 15 minutes, then decrease the oven temperature to 350°F and bake for 30 to 40 minutes longer, until the fruit mixture is thick and bubbling and the crust is browned. Allow to cool for 10 minutes before serving, or cool completely and rewarm to serve.

"When our daughter was little, we'd always go to the Walnut Room for a Christmas lunch. It was quite the scene: the tree, the crowds, and Lanie's favorite part, the costumed characters roaming around blowing fairy dust on all the kids."

Elizabeth Brown has put her stamp on more than fifteen hundred Marshall Field's recipes. As a corporate executive chef, she oversees menu development for Marketplace Foods, Housewares, and Retail Foods. After graduating from the Culinary Institute of America, she cooked in Philadelphia at the Ritz-Carlton and the White Dog Cafe, where she learned firsthand how using seasonal, local, and organic ingredients can benefit both a menu and a community. Elizabeth has tried to bring that philosophy to her recipe development at Field's. She believes that food doesn't have to be fussy or complicated to be deeply satisfying. "Any dish tastes better when it is made with ingredients that are grown nearby," she says, "especially when those ingredients are grown by someone you know." Elizabeth is a coauthor of *The White Dog Cafe Cookbook*.

ANCHO-CHERRY BBQ CHICKEN POTPIE

Serves 4 to 6 | *The unbeatable combo of barbecue and cornbread inspired this family-friendly cross between chicken potpie and tamale pie, with a sweet-spicy BBQ chicken filling and an easy cornbread crust.*

Elizabeth's fresh take on Mrs. Hering's Potpie, page 65

TO PREPARE THE TOPPING, combine the flour, cornmeal, granulated sugar, and baking powder in a small bowl. Add the milk, egg white, and oil and mix until the dough just comes together.

Preheat the oven to 400°F. Place a large saucepan over medium-high heat and add the oil. When the oil is hot, add the onion and cook for about 5 minutes. Add garlic and cook for 2 minutes. Add the chile powder, cumin, coriander, and paprika and toss for 2 minutes. Stir in the ketchup, vinegar, brown sugar, cherries, chicken, and broth and bring to a simmer. Decrease the heat to medium and simmer for about 15 minutes, until thickened. Add the salt and pepper and taste for seasoning. Stir in the cream.

Pour the chicken mixture into an 8- or 9-inch pie pan. Use a rubber spatula to spread the cornbread mixture evenly over the top. Bake for 20 to 25 minutes, until the cornbread is cooked through and the filling is bubbling. Serve warm.

CORNBREAD TOPPING

10 tablespoons all-purpose flour

6 tablespoons cornmeal

2 tablespoons granulated sugar

1 teaspoon baking powder

1/2 cup milk

1 egg white

2 tablespoons vegetable oil

2 tablespoons vegetable oil

1 1/2 cups diced onion

1 tablespoon minced garlic

1 tablespoon dried ancho chile powder

2 teaspoons ground cumin

2 teaspoons ground coriander

1 1/2 teaspoons paprika

1 cup ketchup

1/3 cup apple cider vinegar

1/3 cup brown sugar

3/4 cup dried tart cherries, roughly chopped

3 cups shredded roasted chicken

2 cups low-sodium chicken broth

2 teaspoons salt

1/2 teaspoons freshly ground black pepper

1/2 cup heavy whipping cream

WILD MUSHROOM PESTO PASTA

Serves 4 | *If you like the make-ahead convenience and robust flavor of pasta with pesto sauce, try Elizabeth's version made with a mixture of wild and cultivated mushrooms, roasted to bring out their meaty flavor. You can find truffle oil in specialty foods stores. It's an expensive luxury ingredient, but a little goes a long way. For an easy hors d'oeuvre, you can make crostini by spreading the pesto on thin rounds of toasted baguette.*

Preheat the oven to 400°F.

Toss the mushrooms in a large bowl with the sherry, olive oil, soy sauce, and pepper. Spread out on a baking sheet in an even layer, making sure the mushrooms aren't too crowded. Roast for 30 minutes, until the mushrooms turn golden and have given up their juices. Remove from the oven and allow to cool to room temperature. Transfer the mushrooms and any accumulated juices to the bowl of a food processor.

Add the pine nuts, roasted garlic, and Parmesan to the food processor and pulse to a coarse purée. Remove the lid, scrape down the sides, and add the parsley, rosemary, and lemon juice. With the motor running, pour in the extra virgin olive oil. Transfer to a bowl, adjust the seasoning as necessary, and stir in the truffle oil.

Bring a large pot of salted water to a rolling boil. Add the pasta and cook according to the package instructions. Drain the pasta, reserving 1 cup of the cooking liquid.

Place the pasta in a large bowl. Add the mushroom pesto and reserved cooking liquid and toss until well combined. Taste and adjust the seasoning as necessary. Serve at once, with an extra drizzle of white truffle oil if desired.

1 pound mixed wild, cremini, and button mushrooms

1/4 cup dry sherry

2 tablespoons olive oil

1 1/2 tablespoons soy sauce

1/4 teaspoon freshly ground black pepper

1/4 cup pine nuts, toasted (see page 68)

1/4 head (about 6 medium cloves) roasted garlic (see page 61)

1/2 cup freshly grated Parmesan cheese

1/4 cup finely chopped fresh flat-leaf parsley

1 teaspoon finely chopped fresh rosemary leaves

1 teaspoon freshly squeezed lemon juice

1/4 cup extra virgin olive oil

1 tablespoon white truffle oil, plus more for serving

1 pound angel hair pasta

APPLE, CHICKEN, AND ENDIVE CHOPPED SALAD

Serves 4

"Chopped salads are one of my favorite ways to showcase the bounty of each season—fresh corn, tomatoes, basil, and bacon in the summer; asparagus, fava beans, mint, and prosciutto in the spring; oranges, fennel, beets, and olives in mid-winter; and this combination of greens, chicken, fruit, nuts, bacon, goat cheese, and a sweet maple vinaigrette in the fall," says Elizabeth. "This recipe works well with leftover turkey and any kind of nuts and dried fruit—raisins, currants, cherries, or whatever you've got in the pantry."

Elizabeth's fresh take on Chopped Salad with White Balsamic Vinaigrette, page 43

TO PREPARE THE VINAIGRETTE, combine the vinegar, shallot, maple syrup, mustard, and thyme in a blender and process to combine. With the motor running, pour in the oils in a slow, steady stream. Stir in the salt and pepper, then taste and adjust the seasoning as necessary. Use immediately or cover and refrigerate for up to 3 days.

Place a large skillet over medium-high heat. Add the bacon and cook, turning, until crisped. Transfer to paper towels to drain and cool. Crumble the bacon.

Combine the bacon, apples, chicken, cranberries, pistachios, endive, spinach, and goat cheese in a large bowl and toss well. Just before serving, toss with ¹/₂ cup of the vinaigrette.

"Roasted chicken is one of my secret weapons. I just go ahead and buy two: one for tonight and one to use in salads and other stuff later in the week."

MAPLE VINAIGRETTE

¹/₃ cup apple cider vinegar

2 tablespoons minced shallot

2 tablespoons pure maple syrup

2 teaspoons Dijon mustard

1¹/₂ teaspoons chopped fresh thyme leaves

¹/₃ cup walnut oil

¹/₃ cup olive oil

1 teaspoons salt

¹/₂ teaspoon freshly ground black pepper

4 slices bacon

1 large Granny Smith apple, diced (about 1¹/₂ cups)

1 large Braeburn or other red-skinned apple, diced (about 1¹/₂ cups)

1 roasted chicken, meat removed and chopped (about 3 cups)

1 cup dried cranberries

¹/₂ cup pistachios, toasted and chopped (see page 32)

4 cups thinly sliced endive

4 cups thinly sliced spinach

6 ounces goat cheese, crumbled

SOUR CREAM–CRANBERRY COFFEE CAKE

Serves 8 to 10 | *When Elizabeth's mom was a young bride who had just married a minister, an elderly church member passed this recipe along to her. It's one her family still treasures—a classic American coffee cake, ultra-moist and rich, with a nutty, brown sugar layer in the center. In the summer, Elizabeth likes to substitute fresh blueberries and sliced almonds for the cranberries and pecans.*

Preheat the oven to 350°F. Grease a 10-cup, fluted, nonstick Bundt pan with nonstick spray.

Combine the melted butter, sugar, eggs, sour cream, and vanilla in a large bowl and mix well. Stir in the flour, wheat germ, salt, and baking powder and mix until just combined; do not overmix. Fold in the cranberries.

In a separate bowl, combine the pecans, brown sugar, and cinnamon and toss to mix well.

Pour half of the batter into the prepared pan. Sprinkle on the nut mixture. Cover with the remaining batter. Bake for 50 to 60 minutes, until firm and golden brown on top. Allow to cool for 10 minutes before inverting onto a plate to unmold.

1 cup unsalted butter, melted and slightly cooled

2 cups granulated sugar

2 eggs, beaten

1 cup sour cream

1 teaspoon pure vanilla extract

1 1/2 cups all-purpose flour

1/4 cup wheat germ

1 teaspoon table salt (not kosher salt)

1 teaspoon baking powder

2 scant cups fresh cranberries, roughly chopped

1/2 cup chopped pecans

1 tablespoon dark brown sugar

1 teaspoon ground cinnamon

Tom Douglas and his wife, Jackie Cross, are the creative forces behind four of the most remarkable restaurants in Seattle. Tom started cooking in his native Delaware before heading west to Seattle in the late seventies. Along the way, he tried his hand at everything from building houses and selling wine to repairing railroad cars—dining out across America and Europe all the while, and storing away taste memories to create his own original interpretations. His eclectic style proved a perfect fit for the emerging Pacific Rim cuisine of the Northwest, which combines traditions and flavors from Asia, Alaska, Canada, and California with the abundant seafood and fresh ingredients of the region. It all comes together at his wildly popular restaurants— Dahlia Lounge, Etta's, Palace Kitchen, and Lola—and in his cookbooks—*Tom's Big Dinners*, *Tom Douglas' Seattle Kitchen*, and *I Love Crabcakes*.

WILD MUSHROOM POTPIES

Serves 4

Pine forests, rain, and fog are the perfect recipe for wild mushrooms. No wonder they're such a staple of Pacific Northwest cooking. Tom's potpie is a meatless mélange of wild mushrooms (you can throw in some cultivated ones, too), potatoes, spinach, and corn. Each serving is topped with an individual pastry lid that's baked separately.

Tom's fresh take on Mrs. Hering's Potpie, page 65

TO PREPARE PASTRY, combine the flour and salt in a food processor. Add the butter and pulse a few times until crumbs form. Transfer to a bowl and add the ice water 1 to 2 tablespoons at a time, mixing with a fork or rubber spatula until the dough is just moist enough to hold together. Form the dough into a flattened round, wrap tightly in plastic wrap, and refrigerate for at least 1 hour or overnight.

Preheat the oven to 400°F and line a baking sheet with parchment paper. In a small bowl, whisk together the egg yolk and cold water. Divide the dough into 4 pieces. On a lightly floured surface, roll each piece of dough out into a circle about 7 inches round and 1/8 inch thick. Trim the rounds to make 6-inch circles. Set the pastry circles on the prepared baking sheet and brush with the egg wash. Bake for 12 to 15 minutes, until golden brown.

TO PREPARE THE FILLING, bring a pot of water to a boil. Add the potatoes and cook for 6 to 8 minutes, until tender. Drain the potatoes. Melt the butter in a large, wide pan over medium-high heat. Add the mushrooms, onion, celery, garlic, thyme, and sage and sauté for 8 to 10 minutes, until the vegetables are soft and there is a little browning on the bottom of the pan. Add the wine and bring to a boil, scraping up any browned bits from the bottom of the pan. Boil for 4 to 6 minutes, until the wine is reduced to a glaze. Add the cream and simmer for 5 to 10 minutes, until slightly reduced. Add the potatoes, spinach, and corn and cook for 3 to 4 minutes until the spinach is wilted. Season with the salt and pepper. Scoop the filling into 4 wide, shallow bowls. Top each with a warm pastry lid and serve at once.

PASTRY

1 1/4 cups all-purpose flour

1/2 teaspoon salt

1/2 cup cold unsalted butter, diced

About 1/4 cup ice water

1 large egg yolk

1 tablespoon cold water

FILLING

1 pound Yukon Gold potatoes, diced

1 cup unsalted butter

1 3/4 pounds shiitake, oyster, chanterelle, black trumpet, portobello, or morel mushrooms, thickly sliced, any assortment

1 medium onion, diced

3 celery stalks, diagonally sliced (about 1 1/4 cup)

4 cloves garlic, sliced

2 tablespoons chopped fresh thyme leaves

1 tablespoon chopped fresh sage

1 cup white wine

2 1/2 cups heavy whipping cream

1 cup fresh spinach

1/3 cup fresh corn kernels

3/4 tablespoon salt

3 pinches freshly ground black pepper

MOM'S SHRIMP SALAD ON POTATO CHIPS

Serves 8 to 10

Tom's mom made a delicious creamy shrimp salad with a Thousand Island–style dressing that the whole family loved. She would spoon the salad onto Ritz crackers, but he likes to serve it on potato chips as a chip-and-dip-style appetizer that's great with drinks or beer. You can make your own homemade potato chips, like Tom does, or just buy top-quality chips.

Tom's fresh take on Shrimp Salad Sandwich on Toasted Cheese Bread, page 52

In a large bowl, whisk the tomato paste and honey together until smooth. Whisk in the mayonnaise, chives, lemon juice, cherry pepper, lemon zest, horseradish, and Tabasco sauce. Using a rubber spatula, gently fold in the egg. Add the shrimp to the bowl and toss it with the dressing. Season to taste with salt and pepper and a squeeze of lemon.

Set a bowl of shrimp salad on a large platter and surround it with potato chips for dipping.

3 tablespoons tomato paste

1 tablespoon honey

3/4 cup homemade or store-bought mayonnaise

2 tablespoons thinly sliced chives

1 tablespoon fresh lemon juice

1 tablespoon seeded and minced sweet red cherry pepper (vinegar-packed)

2 teaspoons grated lemon zest

1 teaspoon prepared horseradish

1/4 teaspoon Tabasco sauce

1 hard-boiled egg, finely chopped

1 pound cooked, peeled, and diced shrimp or bay shrimp

Kosher salt and cracked black pepper

1/2 lemon

Potato chips, homemade or store-bought, for serving

CRAB CAKE BLT SANDWICHES

Serves 6

"The only thing more delicious than a crab cake," says Tom, "is a crab cake sandwich with crispy bacon!"
These crab cakes are extra large, so you'll need a wide spatula to flip them in one piece. Dungeness
is the Northwest crab of choice, but you can use whatever variety is locally available, such as blue crab.
If your crabmeat is on the wet side, squeeze out and discard the excess liquid.

TO PREPARE THE CRAB CAKES, tear up the bread and pulse in a food processor to make fine, soft crumbs (you should have about 5 cups). Transfer the bread crumbs to a shallow pan and mix in $^1/_2$ cup of the parsley.

In a food processor, combine the egg yolk, lemon juice, Worcestershire sauce, Tabasco sauce, mustard, paprika, thyme, celery seeds, and black pepper. Pulse to combine. With the motor running, add the oil through the feed tube in a slow, steady stream until the mixture emulsifies and forms a mayonnaise. Transfer the mayonnaise to a bowl.

In a large bowl, combine the onion and bell peppers with the remaining $^1/_4$ cup parsley. Add the mayonnaise and crabmeat and mix lightly. Using a rubber spatula, fold in 1 cup of the bread crumb mixture. Do not over-work the mixture or the crab cakes may get gummy. Gently form 6 cakes and flatten them into patties about $^1/_2$ inch thick. Dredge the patties lightly in the remaining bread crumb mixture. If you have time, cover the crab cakes with plastic wrap and refrigerate for 1 hour or longer.

TO PREPARE THE MAYONNAISE, combine all the ingredients in a small bowl and mix well. Taste and adjust the seasoning with salt as necessary. Cover and refrigerate.

Preheat the oven to 400°F. Put the bacon on a baking sheet, place it in the oven, and cook until crisp, 8 to 10 minutes. Remove the bacon from the pan and drain on paper towels.

Place 2 large, nonstick skillets over medium heat and add about 2 table-spoons of the butter to each pan. Add 3 crab cakes to each pan and slowly fry them for 4 to 5 minutes on each side, until they are golden brown and heated through.

CRAB CAKES

5 to 6 slices white sandwich bread

$^3/_4$ cup chopped fresh parsley

1 large egg yolk

2 teaspoons freshly squeezed lemon juice

2 teaspoons Worcestershire sauce

$1^1/_2$ teaspoons Tabasco sauce

2 tablespoons plus 1 teaspoon Dijon mustard

$^1/_2$ teaspoon paprika

$^1/_2$ teaspoon chopped fresh or dried thyme

$^1/_2$ teaspoon celery seeds

$^1/_4$ teaspoon freshly ground black pepper

5 tablespoons olive oil

$^1/_4$ cup chopped onion

$^1/_4$ cup chopped green bell pepper

$^1/_4$ cup chopped red bell pepper

1 pound Dungeness crabmeat, picked over and drained

HORSERADISH MAYONNAISE

1 cup mayonnaise

2 tablespoons prepared horseradish

2 tablespoons freshly squeezed lemon juice

2 teaspoons grated lemon zest

$^1/_8$ teaspoon freshly ground black pepper

Kosher salt

Preheat the broiler. Place the bread on a baking sheet and toast under the broiler, turning, until light golden brown on both sides. Lightly spread each slice of bread with the horseradish mayo. Put the cooked bacon on a baking sheet and warm it briefly under the broiler.

Place 1 slice of toast, mayo side up, on each plate. Top each with 1 crab cake, 3 pieces of bacon, a tomato slice, and lettuce leaves. Place a second slice of toast on top, mayo side down.

18 slices thick-cut bacon (a little more than 1 pound)

About 4 tablespoons unsalted butter

12 slices firm white sandwich bread, such as Pepperidge Farm

6 slices tomato

6 butter lettuce leaves

BAY BRANDIED BING CHERRIES

Serves 4 to 6

During cherry season, Tom and his family drive out to the Yakima Valley town of Prosser to help their friends, the owners of Chinook Winery, pick all the sweet cherries from their trees. Here's one of the ways he likes to use them—a quick dessert sauce of sweet cherries in brandy syrup with bay leaves. "Spoon the cherries and their syrup over a scoop of ice cream or a slice of pound cake," he suggests, "or drop one into a Manhattan instead of a maraschino."

Combine the sugar and water in a heavy saucepan over medium-high heat. Bring to a boil, stirring to dissolve the sugar. Add the cherries, bay leaves, and $1/4$ cup of the Cognac, decrease the heat to medium, and simmer for 10 minutes. Remove from the heat and strain the cherries from the cooking liquid, reserving both the cherries and the liquid. Put the cherries and bay leaves in a heat-proof bowl and return the liquid to the saucepan.

Bring the liquid to a boil over medium-high heat and continue to boil for 5 minutes, until syrupy and reduced to $1/2$ cup. Remove the pan from the heat and pour the hot syrup over the cherries. Allow the brandied cherries to cool, then stir in the remaining $1/4$ cup Cognac. You can set the bowl of cherries over a bowl of ice water to cool them more quickly, if desired. Remove and discard the bay leaves before serving. The cherries can be covered and refrigerated for up to a few weeks; the flavor mellows and improves after a few days.

$2/3$ cup sugar

$1/2$ cup water

1 pound whole Bing or other sweet cherries, stemmed and pitted

2 bay leaves

$1/2$ cup Cognac or other good-quality brandy

"I've always been a booster of using the local and seasonal ingredients of the Pacific Northwest, both in my restaurants and at home, and Washington State cherries are one of my top favorites."

Todd English got his first restaurant job when he was fifteen and never looked back. In 1982, he graduated from the Culinary Institute of America and, after cooking under Jean-Jacques Rachou at New York's La Côte Basque, he traveled to Italy to apprentice at two famous restaurants, dal Pescatore and Paracucchi. He drew on that experience and his own Italian heritage to develop his now-famous style of cooking—an inventive blend of Mediterranean influences, bold flavors, and luxury ingredients he has described as "refined rustic." When he opened Olives restaurant in Charlestown, Massachusetts, in 1989, it was an instant sensation. A branchful of other Olive's followed in New York, Washington DC, Aspen, and Las Vegas, along with other renowned restaurants in Boston, Seattle, and Orlando. New additions are slated to open in 2006 in New Orleans, Biloxi, and Los Angeles. Todd is the author of three acclaimed cookbooks and appears frequently on national television.

CONFIT TURKEY POTPIES with Cranberry-Orange Compote

Serves 4

Here's a stellar example of Todd's "refined rustic" approach. Potpies, yes, but with a filling of succulent turkey confit (turkey slowly simmered in duck fat) and vegetables. The ruby color and bright, tangy flavor of the cranberry-orange compote make a nice contrast to the velvety richness of the pies. If you're pressed for time, use leftover turkey or rotisserie chicken instead of the turkey confit.

Todd's fresh take on Mrs. Hering's Potpie, page 65

TO PREPARE THE TURKEY, melt the duck fat in a sauté pan over medium heat. Add the turkey thighs, orange, and rosemary. Decrease the heat to low, cover tightly, and cook for about 2 hours, until the turkey falls off the bone. Allow the meat to cool, then pull from the bones and shred or chop into bite-size pieces, discarding the bones and skin.

TO PREPARE THE COMPOTE, combine the cranberries, orange juice, orange zest, and sugar in a saucepan over medium heat. Simmer for 20 to 25 minutes, until the berries break down and the juice evaporates.

TO PREPARE THE PASTRY, whisk the egg and milk together in a small bowl. Lightly brush the egg wash over the puff pastry. Dot the top with the butter. Season with the rosemary, garlic, and pepper. Cut the pastry into four 5-inch circles. Score each dough round in a grid pattern with the tip of a sharp knife.

TURKEY CONFIT

2 pounds duck fat

$1^1/_2$ pounds bone-in turkey thighs

1 orange, halved

3 sprigs rosemary

CRANBERRY-ORANGE COMPOTE

2 cups cranberries

1 cup freshly squeezed orange juice

Zest of 1 orange

$^1/_4$ cup sugar

PASTRY

1 egg

$^1/_4$ cup milk

1 sheet frozen puff pastry, thawed

2 tablespoons unsalted butter

1 tablespoon chopped fresh rosemary leaves

1 tablespoon chopped garlic

Freshly cracked black pepper

TO PREPARE THE FILLING, melt the butter in a sauté pan over medium heat. Add the celery, carrots, onions, mushrooms, and rosemary and sauté for about 8 minutes, until soft. Add the wine and deglaze, scraping up any browned bits from the bottom of the pan. Sprinkle in the flour. Add the broth and bring to a simmer. Add the turkey meat and peas and season to taste with salt and pepper. Simmer for about 15 minutes, until reduced enough to coat a spoon.

Preheat the oven to 400°F. Divide the filling among four 5-inch cast-iron pans or ramekins and top each with a round of puff pastry. Bake for 15 minutes, until golden brown.

Garnish the potpies with the compote and orange segments and serve at once.

TURKEY FILLING

$1/2$ cup unsalted butter

2 celery stalks, diced

2 carrots, diced

2 onions, diced

8 ounces chanterelle mushrooms

1 tablespoon chopped fresh rosemary leaves

1 cup white wine

$1/4$ cup all-purpose flour

3 cups chicken broth

1 cup frozen peas

Salt and freshly ground black pepper

2 oranges, peeled and sectioned, for garnish

"The platter's the canvas. It should express the food without calling too much attention to itself. Complex food presented in a rustic way is very cool. I like serving on chopping blocks and boards."

MUSHROOM-CRUSTED SIRLOIN with Gorgonzola Couscous

Serves 4

These club-cut (meaning thick and narrow) sirloin steaks are topped with a rich mushroom pâté—a presentation based on a porcini-crusted filet that Todd came up with at Olives. If you can't get club-cut sirloin, New York strip or filet mignon will also work well. "This is not your average weeknight recipe," he says. "It's more of a special occasion thing. Great for entertaining." If you're preparing it for a dinner party, use the tried-and-true restaurant technique that Todd suggests in the recipe: cook and top the steaks up to a day ahead and rewarm them in the oven just before serving.

Todd's fresh take on Mushroom-Crusted Sirloin Steak, page 67

TO PREPARE COUSCOUS, melt the butter in a saucepan over medium heat. Add the leek and cook for 3 to 4 minutes, until soft. Add the broth and bring to a boil. Stir in the couscous and cook at a rolling boil for 1 minute, then cover and remove from the heat. Allow to rest for 20 minutes, until the liquid is all absorbed. Place the pan over low heat and stir in the cream and cheese. Season to taste with salt and pepper.

Place a sauté pan over medium-high heat and add the oil. Season both sides of the steaks with salt and pepper. Place the steaks in the pan and sear, turning once, for 4 to 5 minutes on each side. Remove from the pan and arrange on a baking sheet.

TO PREPARE THE CRUST, heat a large sauté pan over medium heat and add the oil. When the oil is hot, add the mushrooms and sear for 6 to 8 minutes, until brown. Transfer the mushrooms to the bowl of a food processor. Add the shallots, garlic, and thyme to the pan and cook for 1 minute. Add the brandy to the pan to deglaze, scraping up any browned bits on the bottom of the pan. Cook for 1 minute, until the brandy has reduced. Add the vinegar and cook for 2 minutes, until reduced. Add the cream and cook for 4 to 5 minutes, until thickened.

continued

GORGONZOLA COUSCOUS

2 tablespoons unsalted butter

1 small leek, trimmed, washed, and diced

2 cups chicken broth

2 cups Israeli couscous, toasted

1/2 cup heavy whipping cream

4 ounces crumbled Gorgonzola cheese

Salt and freshly ground black pepper

2 tablespoons extra virgin olive oil

4 (8-ounce) club-cut sirloin steaks

Salt and freshly ground black pepper

MUSHROOM CRUST

3 tablespoons extra virgin olive oil

8 ounces shiitake mushrooms, sliced

2 shallots, minced

2 cloves garlic, chopped

4 thyme sprigs, chopped

2 ounces brandy

2 tablespoons sherry vinegar

1 cup heavy whipping cream

Salt and freshly ground black pepper

2 tablespoons chopped fresh parsley

Immediately transfer the mixture to the food processor with the mushrooms. Pulse to combine, leaving it somewhat chunky. Season to taste with salt and pepper and stir in the parsley. Spread the warm mushroom mixture evenly over the 4 seared steaks. (The steaks may be prepared to this point up to 24 hours in advance, and kept refrigerated. Bring them to room temperature before proceeding, and increase the warming time to about 12 minutes for medium-rare doneness.)

Preheat the oven to 400°F. Place the steaks in the oven for 3 to 5 minutes, until warmed through and cooked to desired doneness. Serve at once with the couscous alongside.

CAST-IRON ROASTED ZUCCHINI

Serves 4 to 6

Todd likes to serve this homey side dish with roast chicken or fish. "My mom used to make it all the time when I was growing up," he says. "Sometimes she'd throw in potatoes or beans. Sometimes she'd dice the zucchini a little smaller and turn it into a pasta sauce." Don't be scared off by the anchovies. They melt into the mix and add a deep, intense flavor that's anything but fishy.

Place a large, cast-iron skillet over medium-high heat and when it is hot, add the oil. Add the anchovies, garlic, and onion. Cook for 4 to 6 minutes, until the onions brown. Add the zucchini and cook until lightly browned, about 10 minutes. Stir in the tomatoes, wine, oregano, pepper flakes, and salt and pepper to taste. Decrease the heat to medium-low and cook at a low simmer until the zucchini is soft but still holds its shape, about 45 minutes.

Transfer to a serving bowl and garnish with the parsley and Parmesan. Serve warm.

"Most food tastes best at body temperature."

2 tablespoons extra virgin olive oil

2 anchovy fillets, chopped

4 cloves garlic, thinly sliced

1 onion, diced

4 zucchini, thickly sliced

2 cups canned crushed tomatoes

$1/2$ cup dry white wine

1 tablespoon chopped fresh oregano leaves

$1/2$ teaspoon crushed red pepper flakes

Salt and freshly ground black pepper

2 tablespoons chopped fresh parsley, for garnish

$1/2$ cup shaved Parmesan cheese, for garnish

MARINATED SALMON with Eggplant Mash and Pomegranate Vinaigrette

Serves 4

Tandoori spice and yogurt are the secrets to this easy, Indian-inspired fish that forms a bright red, spicy crust as it grills. Look for tandoori spice (you want the powder, not the paste for this recipe) in Indian groceries and some supermarkets. Todd recommends using meaty, oily fish like salmon, halibut, or bluefish, which absorb the flavors of the marinade best. He serves the fish with a salad of thinly sliced cucumbers and suggests basmati rice or Indian naan bread as an accompaniment if you don't have time to make the eggplant mash.

Combine the yogurt, honey, lemon juice, tandoori spice, and ginger in a bowl and mix well. Place the salmon in a shallow baking dish and pour the marinade over, turning to coat evenly. Cover and place in the refrigerator for 4 hours.

TO PREPARE THE EGGPLANT MASH, preheat the oven to 350°F. Place the eggplant in a baking dish and roast for 45 minutes, until soft on the inside. Remove from the oven and allow to cool completely. Scoop out the pulp onto a cutting board and chop well. Place a sauté pan over medium-high heat and add the oil. When the oil is hot, add the onion and sauté for 3 to 4 minutes, until soft. Add the eggplant and cook until the mixture is a chunky mash. Stir in the lemon juice and season to taste with salt and pepper.

TO PREPARE THE VINAIGRETTE, whisk the shallots, green onion, molasses, pomegranate seeds, orange juice, and oil together in a small bowl. Season with salt and pepper to taste.

Preheat a gas grill to high or prepare a hot fire in a charcoal grill. Remove the salmon from the marinade and dry with paper towels. Spray the grill rack with nonstick spray. Place the salmon on the grill rack and cook, turning once, for about 4 minutes on each side, to desired doneness.

To serve, place a scoop of the eggplant mash in the middle of each plate. Place a piece of salmon on top and drizzle with the vinaigrette. Serve at once.

2 cups yogurt

3 tablespoons honey

2 tablespoons freshly squeezed lemon juice

2 tablespoons tandoori spice

2 tablespoons chopped fresh ginger

Salt and freshly ground black pepper

4 (6-ounce) salmon fillets

EGGPLANT MASH

3 small Italian eggplants

2 tablespoons extra virgin olive oil

1 small onion, diced

Juice of 1 lemon

Salt and freshly ground black pepper

POMEGRANATE VINAIGRETTE

2 tablespoons chopped shallots

2 tablespoons sliced green onion

2 tablespoons pomegranate molasses

Seeds from $1/2$ pomegranate

1 tablespoon freshly squeezed orange juice

$1/4$ cup extra virgin olive oil

Salt and freshly ground black pepper

Tyler Florence is all about keeping it real in the kitchen—with bright flavors, uncomplicated recipes, and bold, fresh food. As the host of numerous Food Network programs, including *Food 911, How to Boil Water,* and *Tyler's Ultimate,* and the author of *Tyler Florence's Real Kitchen* and *Eat This Book: Cooking with Global Fresh Flavors,* he combines simple techniques, practical advice, and a generous helping of humor and charisma to create everyday food with extraordinary flavor and appeal. After graduating from the College of Culinary Arts at Johnson and Wales University in South Carolina, he set his sights on New York, where he worked under some of the city's premier chefs, including Charlie Palmer at Aureole, Marta Pulini at Mad 61, and Rick Laakonen at the River Café, before making a name for himself at Cibo and Cafeteria.

CHICKEN AND FRESH VEGETABLE POTPIES

Serves 4

"Simple is good. Tradition is good. Start there, add a little touch of your own, and you're golden," says Tyler. Case in point: his classic potpies, made with tender chunks of chicken, carrots, pearl onions, and sweet peas, with a contemporary twist—an easy Parmesan–puff pastry crust.

Tyler's fresh take on Mrs. Hering's Potpie, page 65

TO PREPARE THE BROTH, tie the thyme, rosemary, and bay leaf together with kitchen twine. Put the chicken in a large stockpot and cover with 1 gallon of cool water. Add the carrots, celery, onion, garlic, turnips, and herb bundle and bring to a boil over medium-high heat. Skim well and then simmer uncovered for 45 minutes, skimming frequently, until the chicken is cooked through. Transfer the chicken to a platter. Continue simmering the broth for another 15 minutes to condense the flavor; you should have about 8 cups. Using a colander, strain the broth into another pot and discard the solids. When the chicken is cool enough to handle, shred the meat and discard the skin and bones.

Bring a small saucepan full of salted water to a boil over high heat. Add the onions and peas and blanch for 2 minutes. Immediately drain and cool under running water. Pinch the skins off the onions. (You can also use frozen onions and peas, thawed under cool running water for 2 minutes.)

Wipe out the stockpot used for cooking the broth and return it to the stovetop over medium heat. Add the butter and heat until melted. Whisk in the flour to form a paste. Gradually pour in 8 cups of the chicken broth, whisking the entire time to prevent lumps. Whisk and simmer for 10 minutes to cook out the starchy taste of the flour and thicken the broth; it should look like cream of chicken soup. Season with salt and pepper. Add the shredded chicken, onions, peas, carrots, and thyme. Stir to combine and then turn off the heat.

CHICKEN BROTH

4 thyme sprigs

2 rosemary sprigs

1 bay leaf

1 (3-pound) chicken

3 carrots, cut into 2-inch pieces

3 celery stalks, cut into 2-inch pieces

1 onion, halved

1 head garlic, halved horizontally

2 turnips, halved

1 cup fresh pearl onions

1 cup fresh sweet peas

$1/2$ cup unsalted butter

$1/2$ cup all-purpose flour

Sea salt and freshly ground black pepper

4 carrots, cut into $1/2$-inch rounds

Leaves from 4 thyme sprigs

2 sheets frozen puff pastry, thawed

1 egg

3 tablespoons water

$1/4$ cup shredded Parmigiano-Reggiano cheese

Preheat the oven to 350°F. Lay the pastry sheets out on a lightly floured, cool surface. Set out four 12-ounce ramekins or crocks. Invert one of the ramekins on the pastry and cut around it with a sharp knife to form 4 pastry rounds slightly larger than the diameter of the ramekin. Divide the chicken mixture among the ramekins, filling them each three-quarters of the way full. Top each with a pastry round, pressing the dough around the rim to form a seal.

Lightly whisk together the egg and water in a small bowl. Brush the egg wash on the pastry tops, then sprinkle with the cheese. Place the ramekins on a baking sheet and bake for 20 minutes, until puffed and golden. Serve hot.

"Cooking is practice. Make a dish once and you get to know it. Make it twice and you own it. The next time someone comes over, you've got that thing you know you can really pull off, and you look like a rock star in the kitchen."

COLD PASTA SALAD with Roasted Chicken, Plums, Blue Cheese, and Basil

Serves 6

Tyler's a fan of techniques that add flavor and save time—like pan-roasting fresh plums right along with the chicken breasts to make this easy, complex-tasting pasta salad. "Ingredients like blue cheese and fresh basil do the same kind of thing," he adds. "They deliver a ton of flavor without a lot of work."

Tyler's fresh take on Blueberry Chicken Salad with Apples, Grapes, Hazelnuts, and Blue Cheese, page 76

Preheat the oven to 375°F. Place a cast-iron or other oven-proof skillet over medium heat. Pour in enough oil to coat the bottom of the pan and heat until almost smoking. Sprinkle the chicken breasts with a generous amount of salt and pepper and put them in the pan, skin side down. Cook for 5 minutes, until the skin is golden brown. Flip the breasts and cook 5 more minutes. Flip the breasts again so that they're skin side down, place the pan in the oven and roast for 10 minutes, until the chicken is about halfway cooked. Carefully take the pan out of the oven and add the plum halves, cut sides down. Put the pan back in the oven and keep cooking for about 15 more minutes, until the chicken juices run clear and the plums are soft and juicy. Take the chicken and plums out of the pan and stick them in the refrigerator to chill.

Bring a big pot of salted water to a boil over high heat. Add the penne and give it a stir to keep the pasta from sticking together. Boil for 8 to 9 minutes, until al dente. Drain in a colander and chill under cold running water.

TO PREPARE THE VINAIGRETTE, whisk together the mustard, vinegar, and sugar in a large serving bowl. Whisk in the oil and season with salt and pepper. Fold in the chives and parsley.

Remove the chilled chicken from the bone and slice. Slice the plums if they are large or leave them whole. Toss the chicken and plums in the dressing in the bowl along with the chilled pasta, blue cheese, and basil leaves. Toss and taste for seasoning.

Extra virgin olive oil

2 bone-in skin-on chicken breasts

Kosher salt and freshly ground black pepper

1 pound plums, halved and pitted

1 pound penne pasta

VINAIGRETTE

1 tablespoon Dijon mustard

1 teaspoon red wine vinegar

1 teaspoon sugar

1/3 cup extra virgin olive oil

Kosher salt and freshly ground black pepper

1 bunch fresh chives, minced

Handful of parsley leaves, chopped

1/4 pound blue cheese, crumbled

Handful of whole basil leaves

THE ULTIMATE SPAGHETTI AND MEATBALLS

Serves 4 to 6

When it comes to spaghetti and meatballs, here's how Tyler defines ultimate: "Giant, juicy meatballs made with pork, beef, Parmesan, lots of fresh herbs, and bread soaked in milk the old-fashioned Tuscan way. You smother them in a homemade pomodoro sauce, finish them with mozzarella and basil, bake them in the oven, and pile them on a big, family-style mountain of spaghetti. It's like having Robert De Niro and Martin Scorsese on one plate."

TO PREPARE THE SAUCE, heat the olive oil in a large saucepan over medium-low heat. Add the onion and garlic and cook until the vegetables are soft, 4 to 5 minutes. Carefully add the tomatoes (nothing splashes like tomatoes) and about 1/2 cup of the reserved liquid and season with salt and pepper. Cook until the sauce is thickened, about 15 minutes. Taste and adjust the seasoning with salt and pepper. Increase the heat to medium-high, bring to a boil and stir for a few minutes with a wooden spoon to further break up the tomatoes. Decrease the heat and let simmer for 20 to 30 minutes. Stir in the basil and season again.

Heat 3 tablespoons oil in an ovenproof skillet over medium heat. Add the onion, garlic, and parsley and cook until the vegetables are soft but not colored, about 10 minutes. Take the pan off the heat and let cool.

Place the bread in a bowl and pour the milk over it. Let it soak while the onion is cooling. Combine the beef and pork in a separate large bowl. Add the egg and Parmigiano and season generously with salt and pepper. Use your hands to squeeze the excess milk out of the bread and add to the meat along with the cooled onion mixture. (Hang onto the skillet—you'll need it to cook the meatballs.) Gently combine all the ingredients with your hands until just mixed together. Don't overwork the mixture or the meatballs will be tough. Divide into 10 equal pieces and shape into nice looking meatballs.

continued

POMODORO SAUCE
Makes 4 cups

1/2 cup extra virgin olive oil

1 onion, chopped

3 cloves garlic, chopped

2 (28-ounce) cans whole peeled tomatoes, preferably San Marzano, drained and crushed by hand, liquid reserved

Kosher salt and freshly ground black pepper

1/4 cup fresh basil leaves, torn into pieces

Extra virgin olive oil

1 onion, chopped

2 cloves garlic, chopped

2 tablespoons finely chopped fresh parsley

4 thick slices firm white bread, crusts removed, cut into cubes (about 2 cups)

1 cup milk

2 pounds ground beef

The Ultimate Spaghetti and Meatballs continued

Preheat the oven to 350°F. Heat a 3-count of oil in the skillet over medium heat. Add the meatballs in batches and brown on all sides, about 10 minutes. Put the meatballs into a baking dish and spoon about half of the tomato sauce over. Shower with the mozzarella and scatter half of the basil leaves over, then drizzle with olive oil. Put the meatballs in the oven and bake until cooked through, about 30 minutes.

Bring a big pot of salted water to a boil. Add the spaghetti and cook until al dente, 8 to 9 minutes. Drain and transfer to a large serving platter. Pour on the rest of the sauce and toss. Spoon the meatballs on top of the spaghetti and garnish with the rest of the basil leaves. Serve immediately along with extra Parmigiano.

2 pounds ground pork

1 large egg

1/2 cup freshly grated Parmigiano-Reggiano cheese, plus more for serving

Kosher salt and freshly ground black pepper

1/2 pound mozzarella cheese, grated

Leaves from 3 sprigs basil

1 pound spaghetti

"When I'm feeding a lot of friends, instead of making forty different things, I like to do one thing really well and serve it family style. A big, beautiful platter gets people talking and having fun."

PAN-FRIED LAMB CHOPS WITH HARISSA

Serves 4 | *Lamb chops, pan-seared or cooked on the grill, are an easy main course for entertaining. Tyler's spicy Middle Eastern harissa sauce and bulgur salad with fresh figs make lamb chops hotter—and cooler—than ever.*

TO MAKE THE SAUCE, place a small, dry skillet over low heat and add the cumin, coriander, and caraway seeds. Toast for about 2 minutes, until fragrant. Grind the seeds to a powder in spice mill or a clean coffee grinder. In a food processor, combine the ground spices, bell peppers, garlic, chiles, salt, olive oil, and lemon juice and pulse to purée.

TO MAKE THE BULGUR SALAD, pour the boiling water over the bulgur in a bowl. Stir in the salt, lemon juice, and olive oil. Cover with a piece of plastic wrap and let stand for 15 to 20 minutes, until the bulgur is tender and all of the liquid has been absorbed. Wrap the almonds in a tea towel and crush with a rolling pin or a heavy saucepan. Stir into the bulgur, along with the green onions, parsley, and mint, and season to taste with salt and pepper. Scatter the figs on top.

When you're ready to eat, heat 2 tablespoons of olive oil in each of 2 large skillets over medium-high heat. Sprinkle the chops on both sides with salt and pepper. Place the chops in the pans and sear, turning once, for about 2 minutes on each side, until browned on the outside and pink inside. Serve the chops at once with the harissa and bulgur salad alongside.

HARISSA SAUCE

1 teaspoon cumin seeds

1 teaspoon coriander seeds

1 teaspoon caraway seeds

1 (12-ounce) jar roasted red bell peppers, chopped

2 cloves garlic

3 small fresh red chiles, chopped

1 teaspoon kosher salt

3 tablespoons extra virgin olive oil

Juice of 1 lemon

BULGUR WHEAT SALAD

1 cup boiling water

1 cup medium-grind bulgur wheat

1/2 teaspoon kosher salt

Juice of 1 lemon

2 tablespoons extra virgin olive oil

1/2 cup smoked or toasted almonds

6 green onions, trimmed and sliced

1/2 cup chopped fresh flat-leaf parsley

Leaves from 1 bunch fresh mint

Kosher salt and freshly ground black pepper

8 fresh Black Mission figs, halved through the stem ends

1/4 cup extra virgin olive oil

12 fat lamb chops

Kosher salt and cracked black pepper

Gale Gand caught the eye of a *Life* magazine photographer when she was making mud pies at age six. Her confections have been turning heads ever since. As executive pastry chef at TRU in Chicago, she's built a reputation as one of the nation's most acclaimed and inventive pastry artists. Her style—whether she's creating splashy restaurant desserts or recipes for home cooks—combines playful charm with serious satisfaction. She loves to draw on classic American flavors and sweet childhood memories to come up with witty, sophisticated takes on favorite combinations like peanut butter and jelly and root beer floats (she also markets her own line of root beer). The host of Food Network's *Sweet Dreams*, she has written three popular dessert cookbooks: *Gale Gand's Short and Sweet, Gale Gand's Just a Bite,* and *Butter Sugar Flour Eggs.*

CHOCOLATE-CHERRY POTPIES

Serves 10 to 12

Leave it to Gale to reinvent potpie as a dessert! If you're partial to chocolate-covered cherries, check out these individual pies with a luscious chocolate filling, a surprising burst of flavor from whole cherries, and a buttery chocolate crust. They work well for entertaining because they can be made ahead and reheated in the oven at the last minute.

Gale's fresh take on Mrs. Hering's Potpie, page 65

TO PREPARE THE CRUST, combine the baking powder, flour, and cocoa powder in a small bowl and mix well. Combine the butter and sugar in a stand mixer fitted with the paddle attachment and cream on medium-high speed until fluffy. Add the egg yolk and vanilla and mix well. Add the dry ingredients and mix until a firm dough forms. Shape the dough into a disk, wrap in plastic wrap, and refrigerate for 1 hour.

TO PREPARE THE FILLING, preheat the oven to 375°F. Combine the egg yolks, eggs, and sugar in a stand mixer fitted with the whisk attachment. Whip on medium-high speed until fluffy and light. Decrease the speed to low and mix in the chocolate and then the butter.

Using a ladle, divide the filling among ten to twelve 4-ounce ramekins. Gently push 3 to 4 cherries down into each one.

Sprinkle a work surface with cocoa powder. Roll the dough out to about 1/8 inch thick, then cut into 10 to 12 rounds to fit the tops of the ramekins.

Arrange the ramekins on a baking sheet and bake for 6 minutes. Remove the ramekins from the oven but leave the oven on.

Place a round on the top of each potpie and bake for 8 to 10 minutes, until crisp. Remove from the oven and allow to cool slightly before topping with the whipped cream and serving. Or allow to cool completely and rewarm before serving. These potpies should be enjoyed the day they are made.

CRUST

1/4 teaspoon baking powder

1 scant cup all-purpose flour

1/4 cup cocoa powder, preferably Dutch process, plus extra for rolling

9 tablespoons cool unsalted butter, cut into pieces

6 tablespoons sugar

1 egg yolk

1/4 teaspoon pure vanilla extract

FILLING

6 egg yolks

4 eggs

1/4 cup sugar

18 ounces semisweet chocolate, melted

10 tablespoons unsalted butter, melted

1 cup fresh or canned cherries, pitted

Whipped cream, for serving (optional)

DOUBLE CHOCOLATE-PEANUT BUTTER COCOA KRISPY TREATS

Makes 18 bars

Riffing on Marshall Field's famous Frango Rice Krispy Treats, Gale thought it might be fun to up the ante by switching the Rice Krispies to Cocoa Krispies and adding a little peanut butter. She was right on both counts.

Gale's fresh take on Frango Rice Krispy Treats, page 90

Grease a 9 by 13-inch baking pan. Place the cereal in a bowl. Combine the brown sugar and corn syrup in a saucepan over medium-high heat and bring to a boil. Boil for 1 minute then turn the heat off. Stir in the peanut butter then pour over the cereal. Stir immediately to combine and coat. Transfer the mixture to the prepared baking dish and spread it out evenly. Immediately pour the Frango chips over the surface and let them melt slightly. Spread the chocolate out to coat the top (if the chips don't melt, pop the dish into a warm oven for a minute until soft). Let the chocolate harden, then cut into bars.

8 cups chocolate crispy rice cereal (such as Cocoa Krispies)

1 cup packed light brown sugar

1 cup light corn syrup

1 cup creamy or crunchy peanut butter

1 (12-ounce) bag Frango Double Chocolate Baking Chips

"Try serving desserts on big plates. It's like putting a matt around a picture—it really sets the food off beautifully."

POPPY SEED CAKES

Makes 6 dozen cookies

"My mom's side of the family—the baking side—were Hungarian Jews," says Gale, "and this recipe is from my grandma Elsie, who came from that wonderful baking world of poppy seeds, walnuts, dried apricots, and lekvar—a purée of prunes." These simple, buttery, slice-and-bake refrigerator cookies are fun to make—and eat—with kids.

Place the butter and sugar in a stand mixer fitted with the paddle attachment and cream them together. Beat in the egg and vanilla until light and fluffy. In a separate bowl, stir together the poppy seeds, salt, flour, and cinnamon. Add the dry ingredients to the mixer and combine well.

Turn the dough out onto a work surface and roll it into 2 logs, each 9 inches long and $1^1/_2$ inches wide. Wrap in wax paper and refrigerate for 2 hours or overnight.

Preheat the oven to 350°F and grease a baking sheet. Cut the dough into $1/_4$-inch slices and place on the baking sheet. Bake the cookies for 10 to 12 minutes, until light golden brown on the edges.

1 cup unsalted butter

$3/_4$ cup sugar

1 egg

1 teaspoon pure vanilla extract

$1/_3$ cup poppy seeds

$1/_4$ teaspoon salt

$2^1/_4$ cups all-purpose flour

$1/_2$ teaspoon ground cinnamon

"It's good to have a few tools you're completely comfortable with, like a good friend. For me, that would be my great-grandmother's rolling pin. I actually travel with it."

LAMB STEW À LA MARSHALL FIELD'S

Serves 8

"This recipe is my attempt to recreate one of my favorite childhood taste memories," says Gale. She's talking about the tender lamb stew she would order at the Marshall Field's Oak Room in Skokie, Illinois, on her regular Tuesday night dates with her mom from the time she was seven years old. "That was my dish. It came in its own little individual casserole," she remembers. "I loved that."

In a shallow bowl, stir together the salt, pepper, and flour. Add the lamb cubes and toss well. Place a Dutch oven over medium-high heat and add the oil. Add the lamb cubes in batches and cook, turning, for 10 to 12 minutes, until browned on all sides. Add the garlic, parsley, bay leaf, thyme, broth, and wine. Decrease the heat to low, cover, and simmer for 2 hours, until the meat is very tender, adding more broth if needed.

Add the carrots and onions, season with a little salt and pepper, if needed, and continue cooking, covered, for another 20 minutes, until the vegetables are tender. Add the peas and cook for another 10 minutes. Serve in individual crocks.

2 teaspoons salt

1 teaspoon freshly ground black pepper

1 cup all-purpose flour

3 pounds cubed lamb meat for stewing

2 tablespoons vegetable oil

1 clove garlic, minced

2 sprigs parsley

1 bay leaf

1/2 teaspoon dried thyme

1 1/2 cups beef broth, plus more if needed

1/2 cup dry red wine

6 carrots, sliced into coins

2 cups pearl onions, or 8 small onions, peeled and halved

2 cups frozen peas

Andrea Robinson is used to firsts. One of only fourteen women in the world to hold the title Master Sommelier, she was the first woman ever named Best Sommelier in the United States by the Sommelier Society of America. She's also the first appointed Dean of Wine Studies for the French Culinary Institute in New York and was the first woman cellar master for Windows on the World. In five books, two television series, and a DVD series, Andrea's down-to-earth, spirited approach has helped demystify wine for hundreds of thousands of people all over the world. She's also an accomplished chef, who loves to create easy, flavorful recipes expressly designed for pairing with wine—the kind showcased in her recent book, *Everyday Dining with Wine: 125 Wonderful Recipes to Match and Enjoy with Wine.*

INDIVIDUAL SALMON, AND MUSHROOM POTPIES

Serves 4

Salmon's a dinnertime standard at Andrea's house. In fact, for this book she's shared three of her family's favorite salmon recipes. These individual potpies are filled with chunks of fresh salmon, fennel, and mushrooms in a creamy sauce. She likes to pair it with an Alsace Pinot Gris.

▯ Andrea's fresh take on Mrs. Hering's Potpie, page 65

Line a baking sheet with parchment paper. Lightly flour a work surface. With a floured rolling pin, roll out the puff pastry to $^1/_8$ inch thick. Invert a 2-cup ramekin on the pastry and cut around it to form 4 pastry circles, each about 1 inch larger in diameter than the ramekin. Place the circles on the prepared baking sheet, brush with the olive oil, and cover with plastic wrap. Refrigerate for 1 hour, until chilled.

Place the chicken broth and fennel stalks in a saucepan and bring to a boil over high heat. Boil until reduced by half. Remove and discard the fennel. Decrease the heat and keep the broth at a low simmer.

Preheat the oven to 400°F. In a heavy skillet, melt $1^1/_2$ tablespoons of the butter over medium-high heat. Add the chopped fennel, fennel fronds, shallot, and wine. Cook, stirring, for 2 minutes, then decrease the heat to medium. Continue cooking, stirring occasionally, for about 7 minutes, until the fennel is soft. Add the mushrooms and cook, stirring frequently, for about 2 minutes, until the fennel and mushrooms are tender. Add the tarragon and salmon and stir well.

In a small bowl, mix together the milk and cornstarch to dissolve. Whisk into the simmering broth and continue whisking for about 1 minute, until the mixture thickens. Cook, stirring, for 2 more minutes. Season with salt and pepper. Stir $1^1/_2$ cups of the gravy into the salmon mixture.

Divide the salmon mixture evenly among four buttered 2-cup ramekins, but do not overfill. Spoon in some additional gravy and put a pat of the remaining butter in each ramekin. Top each with a pastry circle, curling the edges upward and pressing just inside the lip of the ramekin to seal. Bake on a baking sheet for about 15 minutes, until golden brown.

1 sheet frozen puff pastry, thawed

1 tablespoon olive or vegetable oil

2 (14-ounce) cans low-sodium chicken broth

3 or 4 fennel stalks with fronds

3 tablespoons unsalted butter

$1^1/_2$ cups chopped fresh fennel

1 tablespoon chopped fresh fennel fronds

1 small shallot, minced

$^1/_4$ cup dry white wine

1 cup sliced mushrooms

1 tablespoon finely chopped fresh tarragon or chervil leaves (optional)

$1^1/_2$ pounds skinless salmon fillet, sliced crosswise $^1/_2$ inch thick, then cut into 1-inch pieces

1 cup milk

$^1/_4$ cup cornstarch

Kosher salt and freshly ground black pepper

JOHN'S FIRST-DATE SALMON FILLETS

Serves 2

This almost impossibly easy dish was what Andrea's husband, John, made the first time he cooked for her. It matches beautifully with almost any red wine, according to Andrea, but Pinot Noir was what stole her heart that night. "The thyme makes some amazing flavor fireworks with Pinot, and brings out its earthiness and subtlety," she says. "This dish is so simple to pull off, you can actually have a conversation while making it—which is key on a first date. Plus, it's a really good way to use up some of that dried thyme that would otherwise fossilize in your spice rack."

Cut the salmon fillet into 2 equal portions, brush both sides with olive oil, and sprinkle both sides with salt, pepper, and the thyme.

In a large skillet, heat the 1 tablespoon olive oil and the butter over medium-high heat until the butter foams. Carefully place the fillets in the skillet. Cook without moving for about 2 minutes, until the edges begin to crisp. Decrease the heat to medium and cook for about 1 minute, until the fillets are golden brown. Turn the fillets and continue cooking for 5 to 7 minutes, until medium-rare, adding a few drops of olive oil as needed to prevent sticking. Transfer the fillets to plates and drizzle with balsamic vinegar. Serve immediately.

BALSAMIC VINEGAR REDUCTION: Place 1 cup balsamic vinegar in a small saucepan and bring to a boil over high heat. Decrease the heat to medium and simmer until the vinegar is reduced by half. Pour into a non-reactive container and let cool completely. The reduction can be covered and refrigerated for up to 1 month.

3/4 pound (1-inch-thick) center-cut skinless salmon fillet

1 tablespoon olive oil, plus more for brushing

Kosher salt and freshly ground black pepper

1 1/2 teaspoons dried thyme

1 tablespoon unsalted butter

Aged balsamic vinegar or balsamic vinegar reduction, for drizzling (see note)

"You don't need a lot of wine knowledge to enjoy drinking the stuff. But a little goes a long way toward enhancing your buying power and confidence, and also your fun."

WASABI PEA–CRUSTED SALMON SANDWICH

Serves 4

Andrea studied at the French Culinary Institute in New York, which is right on the edge of Chinatown. "We'd always run over there and pick up wacky ingredients," she says. When she first tasted wasabi peas there, she thought, "Wow, they're crunchy, they're spicy, and they're this amazing shade of green that would be really pretty with salmon." So she threw some into a blender and this simple, stunning dish was born. Look for wasabi peas in the produce section, near the granola and trail mixes, or in the Asian section of many supermarkets. Andrea recommends tasting them before using the full amount called for, because some brands are much hotter than others. She suggests serving this dish with a nice, everyday sparkling wine.

Andrea's fresh take on Almond-Crusted Walleye Sandwich, page 55

TO PREPARE THE MAYONNAISE, combine the mayonnaise, sesame oil, soy sauce, and ginger in a bowl and whisk until well blended. Season to taste with salt and pepper. (The mayonnaise can be covered and refrigerated for up to a week.)

Brush both sides of the salmon fillets with olive oil. Place the peas in a blender and process until they are the consistency of bread crumbs. Spread the ground peas on a plate. Dip one side of the fillets into the peas, pressing gently to evenly coat.

In a large, flat-bottomed, nonstick skillet, heat the 2 tablespoons olive oil and the butter over medium heat. Place the fillets peas side down in the skillet and cook for about 4 minutes, until the crust becomes crisp and starts to brown lightly. Carefully lift the edge of each fillet to check the browning and lower the heat if necessary to prevent burning. Turn the fillets and continue to cook for about 4 minutes, until medium rare. Transfer to a paper towel–lined plate to drain briefly.

Split and toast the rolls. Spread each cut face with some of the Asian mayonnaise. Put a lettuce leaf and a piece of salmon on the bottom half of each roll. Top with the other half of the roll. Serve immediately, passing extra mayonnaise at the table.

ASIAN MAYONNAISE

1 cup mayonnaise

1 tablespoon toasted sesame oil

1 tablespoon soy sauce

1 tablespoon grated fresh ginger

Kosher salt and freshly ground black pepper

4 (6-ounce, 1-inch-thick) skinless salmon fillets

2 tablespoons olive oil, plus more for brushing

$1/2$ cup wasabi-crusted peas

2 tablespoons unsalted butter

4 kaiser rolls or other good quality sandwich rolls

4 leaves lettuce

LINGUINE with Walnuts, Arugula, and Black Olives

Serves 4

When Andrea and her husband come up with new recipes, they often start with the wine they want to enjoy and invent the dish "backward" from there. They created this mostly-from-the-pantry pasta to stand up to a big Cabernet. "It's a simple dish that has a lot going on," Andrea explains. "The black olives have a bitter edge that mimics the slight bitterness of the tannin you get in a big Cab. The arugula and walnuts pick up the oaky toastiness. And the oil and cheese soften the tannins so the fruit can really explode."

Add a tablespoon of salt to a large pot filled with 4 quarts of water. Bring to a boil. Add the pasta and cook according to the package directions until al dente.

While the pasta is cooking, place the walnuts in a large dry skillet over medium heat and cook, shaking the pan frequently, for 3 to 4 minutes, until browned and fragrant. Allow to cool slightly, then chop coarsely.

In the same skillet, heat the 2 tablespoons olive oil over medium heat and add the garlic. Cook, stirring, for about 2 minutes, until the garlic begins to soften and turn golden. Remove from the heat.

Drain the pasta, reserving 1/2 cup of the cooking water, and transfer it to the skillet with the garlic. Return to the stovetop over medium heat. Stir in the arugula and the 1/4 cup extra virgin olive oil and toss to coat the pasta and wilt the arugula. Stir in the walnuts and olives, tossing to combine. If the pasta seems dry, add a little bit of the reserved pasta water to moisten.

Remove the pasta from the heat and drizzle with a few more tablespoons of extra virgin olive oil to taste. Stir in the cheese, adding more to taste, black pepper, and a sprinkling of sea salt. Serve immediately.

3/4 pound linguine fini or other thin, flat noodle

1/3 cup walnut pieces

2 tablespoons olive oil

3 large cloves garlic, finely chopped

2 cups firmly packed baby arugula, washed and dried

1/4 cup extra virgin olive oil, plus more for drizzling

1/3 cup chopped pitted black olives

1/4 cup freshly grated Manchego or Parmigiano-Reggiano cheese, plus more if desired

Freshly ground black pepper

Coarse sea salt (such as fleur de sel)

Marcus Samuelsson is no stranger to crossing borders. Born in Ethiopia, he was adopted by a Swedish couple as a young child and grew up on the west coast of Sweden, where his grandmother, a professional cook, introduced him to the pleasures of cooking at an early age. After training in Sweden, Switzerland, and Austria, he apprenticed at Aquavit, a swank Manhattan restaurant featuring stunningly innovative interpretations of Scandinavian cuisine. Following a stint at the three-star Georges Blanc in Lyon, France, he returned to Aquavit, where he was named executive chef at the tender age of twenty-four. He is now the chef and co-owner of Aquavit and a second New York restaurant, Riingo, which offers an American-Japanese fusion menu. Marcus is the author of *Aquavit and the New Scandinavian Cuisine* and the forthcoming *Africa on My Mind*.

CHICKEN BERBERE PIE

Serves 8

Berbere is a spicy Ethiopian seasoning blend—similar to Indian masala—used to season stews and sauces. For this potpie, Marcus took his inspiration from doro wat, a spicy Ethiopian chicken stew made with berbere, hard-boiled eggs, and lime juice. A buttery piecrust stands in for injera, the classic Ethiopian flatbread that's always served alongside.

Marcus's fresh take on Mrs. Hering's Potpie, page 65

TO PREPARE THE DOUGH, combine the flour, salt, butter, and water in a bowl and mix with your hands until it starts to come together. Transfer the dough to a work surface and knead for 5 minutes. Let the dough rest at room temperature for 30 minutes. On a lightly floured surface, roll the dough out to a 1/2-inch-thick, 10-inch circle.

TO PREPARE THE BERBERE, place the fenugreek seeds in a mortar and pestle or spice grinder and grind to a fine powder. Transfer to a bowl and add the remaining berbere ingredients. Stir until well combined.

TO PREPARE THE FILLING, combine 1 tablespoon of the butter, the onions, and a pinch of salt in a Dutch oven over low heat. Cook, stirring occasionally, for about 15 minutes, until the onions are golden. Add the remaining 7 tablespoons butter, the cardamom, pepper, cloves, garlic, ginger, and 2 tablespoons of the berbere. Cook for about 10 minutes, until onions soften and take on the color of the spices.

PIE DOUGH

2 cups all-purpose flour

1 teaspoon salt

1/2 cup cold unsalted butter, cubed

2 tablespoons cold water

BERBERE

1 teaspoon fenugreek seeds or ground coriander

1 cup ground dried serrano chiles, or 1/2 cup paprika mixed with 1/2 cup chile powder

1/2 cup paprika

2 tablespoons salt

2 teaspoons ground ginger

2 teaspoons onion powder

1 teaspoon ground hulled white cardamom

1 teaspoon ground nutmeg

1/2 teaspoon garlic powder

Add 1 cup of the chicken broth, the chicken legs, and thighs and simmer for 15 minutes. Add the remaining 1 cup chicken broth and the wine and simmer for 10 minutes. Add the chicken breasts and simmer for 20 minutes. Gently fold in the lime juice and whole eggs and simmer for another 5 minutes to warm through. The sauce will be loose and soupy. Season with salt to taste.

Preheat the oven to 300°F. Transfer the filling to a 10-inch pie pan and allow to cool. Place the dough round on top and bake for 25 minutes. Increase the heat to 350°F and bake for 15 minutes, until golden brown. Serve hot.

¹/₄ teaspoon ground cloves

¹/₄ teaspoon ground cinnamon

¹/₄ teaspoon ground allspice

FILLING

¹/₂ cup unsalted butter

2 red onions, diced

Salt

¹/₄ teaspoon ground hulled white cardamom

¹/₄ teaspoon freshly ground black pepper

3 whole cloves

2 cloves garlic, finely chopped

1 inch fresh ginger, chopped

2 cups chicken broth

2 boneless skinless chicken legs

2 boneless skinless chicken thighs, halved

¹/₄ cup red wine

2 boneless skinless chicken breasts, halved

Juice of 1 lime

2 hard-boiled eggs, peeled

"My grandmother, Helga, started cooking for Christmas in October by making her own aquavits and pickled herring. Then in November she'd start in with the cookies. There was always the scent of spices in the air—cardamom, cumin, cinnamon, saffron. By Christmas, the whole house smelled like a gingersnap."

MUSSEL-CARROT SOUP

"Like everybody these days, I want a lot of flavor but I don't have a lot of time," says Marcus. "And I'm always moving fast, so I don't want to feel stuffed." That's why he came up with this quick, light, intensely flavorful mussel soup. "You can also make it with clams," he suggests, "and if you want something a bit more substantial, you can throw in some cooked Israeli couscous or orzo pasta right at the end."

Place a soup pot over medium-high heat and add the oil. Add the shallots, garlic, ginger, and curry powder and sauté for a few minutes, until soft. Add the mussels, wine, and tarragon and cover the pot. Cook for 5 to 8 minutes, until the mussels open. Using tongs, remove the mussels from the pot.

Add the broth and carrot juice to the pot and bring to a boil. Add the mussel juice, sour cream, and lime juice and whisk well until heated through. Season to taste with salt and pepper.

Divide the mussels among soup bowls and pour the broth on top. The soup can be served hot or cold.

2 tablespoons olive oil

2 shallots, chopped

4 cloves garlic, chopped

1 (3-inch) piece ginger

1 tablespoon curry powder

3 pounds mussels, cleaned and debearded

1 cup white wine

2 sprigs tarragon, stems removed

1 cup chicken broth

3 cups carrot juice

2 cups mussel or clam juice

1 tablespoon sour cream

Juice of 2 limes

Salt and freshly ground black pepper

GRAVLAX WITH MUSTARD SAUCE

Serves 10 to 12

If you're a fan of smoked salmon, you'll like gravlax, a cured version you can make right in your refrigerator. "If you want to try something Scandinavian," Marcus says, "gravlax is the most traditional dish of all, and it's a lot easier than you might think." You can also use tuna or sea bass instead of salmon. And don't stop at fish. "I'd make this with beef tenderloin in a heartbeat," says Marcus. "You just cure it whole and then slice it thin like carpaccio."

TO PREPARE THE GRAVLAX, combine the sugar, salt, and peppercorns in a small bowl and mix well. Place the salmon skin side down in a shallow dish and rub a handful of the sugar mixture into both sides of the fish. Sprinkle the salmon with the remaining mixture and cover with the dill. Cover the dish and let stand for 6 hours in a cool spot. Transfer the salmon to the refrigerator and let cure for 36 hours.

TO PREPARE THE SAUCE, combine the two mustards, the sugar, vinegar, coffee, salt, and pepper in a blender. With the motor running, add the oil in a slow, steady stream, blending until the sauce is thick and creamy. Transfer to a bowl and stir in the dill. Cover and refrigerate for at least 4 hours, or overnight, to allow the flavors to marry.

Scrape the seasonings off the gravlax. Slice the gravlax on the diagonal into thin slices, or leave whole so your guests can slice it themselves. Serve with the mustard sauce and bread.

GRAVLAX

1 cup sugar

1/2 cup kosher salt

2 tablespoons cracked white peppercorns

2 1/2 to 3 pounds skin-on salmon fillet, in one piece, pin bones removed

2 to 3 large bunches fresh dill, coarsely chopped, including stems

MUSTARD SAUCE

2 tablespoons honey mustard

1 teaspoon Dijon mustard

2 teaspoons sugar

1 1/2 tablespoons white wine vinegar

1 tablespoon cold strong brewed coffee

Pinch of salt

Pinch of freshly ground black pepper

3/4 cup grapeseed or canola oil

1/2 cup chopped fresh dill

Thin slices potato-mustard bread or whole-grain bread, for serving

TURKEY MEATLOAF with Tomato-Spinach Sauce

Serves 4

"Meatloaf is about as American as it gets," observes Marcus, "and I love it." Recently he wanted to come up with a lighter, leaner version that would still be moist and flavorful. His solution: combining ground turkey with a quick tomato-bell pepper pan sauce. To finish it off, he adds fresh spinach to some of the reserved sauce and serves it over the slices.

Marcus's fresh take on Oven-Baked Meatloaf, page 65

Place a sauté pan over medium-high heat and add the oil. When the oil is hot, add the onion and sauté for 3 minutes, until beginning to soften. Stir in the bell pepper, garlic, and chili powder. Add the tomatoes and thyme, decrease the heat to medium, and simmer for 25 minutes.

Measure out 1 cup of the tomato sauce and spread it on a baking sheet to cool. Let the rest of the tomato sauce continue to simmer over low heat.

Preheat the oven to 300°F. In a bowl, soak the breadcrumbs in the water for 5 to 8 minutes, until they swell. Transfer half of the breadcrumbs to a separate bowl and add the cooled 1 cup tomato sauce, the egg, and ground turkey. Mix well and season with salt and pepper.

Transfer the mixture to a loaf pan and pat to shape. Bake for 1 hour, until the meat is firm and cooked through.

Five minutes before the loaf is ready, fold the rest of the breadcrumbs, the spinach, and basil into the tomato sauce.

To serve, slice the meatloaf and arrange on a serving platter or plates. Pour the remaining tomato sauce over the slices.

3 tablespoons extra virgin olive oil

1 onion, sliced

1 red bell pepper, chopped

4 cloves garlic, minced

1 teaspoon chili powder

8 tomatoes, chopped

4 sprigs thyme, stems removed

1/2 cup fine breadcrumbs

1 cup water

1 pound ground turkey

1 egg

1/2 teaspoon salt

Freshly ground black pepper

2 cups spinach, coarsely chopped

4 sprigs basil, coarsely chopped

"In Sweden, I grew up with the tradition of *husmanskost* or 'home cooking.' It's like a set menu that families follow—about fifteen dishes that you just roll through. Some are tied to days—like Thursday is yellow split pea soup day all over the country. Other dishes like herring, meatballs, and cabbage rolls show up pretty much once a week in every family.

Tim Scott has cooked in restaurants and hotels all over the world. He began his Marshall Field's career as the catering chef and is now the corporate executive chef. Tim creates recipes and menus for twenty full-service restaurants and thirty-five Marketplace outlets in Chicago, Minneapolis, Detroit, and the surrounding areas. He also frequently teaches cooking classes for both adults and children. Tim started cooking professionally at the age of fourteen, and is a graduate of the Culinary Institute of America. He has cooked at many Minneapolis-area restaurants, including Goodfellows and the Nicollet Island Inn, and spent two years at Wolfgang Puck's Postrio in San Francisco. He also worked at the Basel Hilton International in Switzerland and several other restaurants in Cabo San Lucas, New York, Chicago, and Colorado. Tim recently had the honor of cooking at the Sundance Film Festival along with several other Field's Culinary Council chefs.

TURKEY POTPIE TURNOVERS

Serves 8

Tim's turnovers make a tasty point about cooking: little things make a big difference. A few slices of bacon, a handful of wild mushrooms, a splash of sherry, some sliced leeks—ingredients like these can give a classic dish a flavorful, contemporary update. So does Tim's easy idea for making turnovers from frozen pie dough. If you're more of a potpie traditionalist, you can scoop the turkey mixture into ovenproof ramekins, top them with rounds of the pie dough, and bake on a foil-lined baking sheet.

Tim's fresh take on Mrs. Hering's Potpie, page 65

Preheat the oven to 375°F. Place a skillet over medium heat and add the bacon. When the bacon is cooked halfway, add the leeks, carrot, garlic, corn, and mushrooms. Season with salt and pepper to taste. Cook for 3 to 4 minutes, until the vegetables are just done. Transfer to a bowl to cool.

Melt the butter in a saucepan over medium-high heat. Add the flour and whisk to combine. Cook, stirring, for 2 minutes. Add the chicken broth and whisk until smooth. Add the milk and whisk well, making sure there are no lumps. Simmer, stirring occasionally, for 8 minutes. Add the thyme and sherry, season with salt and pepper to taste, and stir well. Remove from the heat.

In a large bowl, combine the vegetables, sauce, and turkey and allow to cool.

Line a baking sheet with parchment paper. In a small bowl, whisk together the egg and water. Place 1 cup of the turkey mixture in each pie shell, just below the center. Brush the egg wash around the edges of the dough. Fold the dough over the filling to form a turnover shape. Crimp or pinch the edges of the dough to seal. Brush each turnover with the egg wash and place them on the prepared baking sheet. Bake for about 20 minutes, until golden brown. Serve hot.

2 slices smoked bacon, cut into
   $1/2$-inch pieces

$1/2$ cup washed sliced leeks
   ($1/4$ inch thick)

1 carrot, diced into $1/2$-inch pieces

2 teaspoons minced garlic

1 cup fresh corn kernels

1 cup morel mushrooms or other wild
   mushrooms, washed and sliced

Kosher salt and freshly ground
   black pepper

4 tablespoons unsalted butter or
   bacon fat

$1/2$ cup all-purpose flour

2 cups chicken broth, warmed

2 cups milk

1 tablespoon fresh thyme leaves

2 tablespoons dry sherry

3 cups roasted turkey, torn into
   bite-size pieces

1 egg

2 tablespoons water

4 (9-inch) frozen pie shells, thawed,
   at room temperature

"I certainly couldn't tell you today what I'm going to eat for dinner tomorrow. I shop for food . . . oh . . . ten times a week. Meat from one place, fish from another. With food that fresh, cooking can be pretty uncomplicated—and really healthy. I just keep it simple and let the ingredients do the heavy lifting."

CHICKEN AND QUINOA SALAD

Serves 4

"Quinoa's been around for thousands of years and it's widely considered to be one of the healthiest grains in the world," says Tim. "It's a complete protein and has a nice crunchy texture. But what it doesn't have much of is flavor." So he simmers it with aromatic vegetables and cinnamon and serves it as a cold salad, topped with spicy grilled chicken, candied walnuts, and a sweet-tart cranberry sauce. "Now, you've got health and flavor, flavor, flavor," he says. For a fancier, restaurant-style presentation, he suggests shaping the salad using a ring mold. The candied walnuts are wonderful on their own and as a topping for other salads and desserts.

Tim's fresh take on Strawberry-Chicken Salad, page 35

Combine the orange juice, chile paste, maple syrup, green onions, and sesame oil in a baking dish and add the chicken, turning to coat evenly. Place in the refrigerator and marinate for at least 30 minutes or no more than 2 hours.

Preheat a gas grill to medium-high or prepare a hot fire in a charcoal grill. Remove the chicken from the marinade and grill, turning once, for 10 to 12 minutes, until cooked through. Allow to cool to room temperature, then refrigerate until completely chilled.

TO PREPARE THE WALNUTS, preheat the oven to 350°F. Lightly coat 2 baking sheets with nonstick spray. Place a perforated steaming basket in a large saucepan over 1 inch of water and bring to a boil over high heat. Place the walnuts in the basket and steam for 1 minute to heat up. Combine the honey and sugar in a bowl. Add the walnuts and toss well. Spread the nuts on 1 of the prepared baking sheets and bake, stirring once or twice, for 10 minutes, until caramelized. Immediately remove from the oven and pour onto the other prepared baking sheet. Allow to cool completely. (The nuts may be stored in a tightly covered container at room temperature for up to 1 week.)

1/2 cup freshly squeezed orange juice

1 teaspoon sambal oelek chile paste (see page 36)

3 tablespoons pure maple syrup

2 tablespoons thinly sliced green onions

1 tablespoon sesame oil

4 boneless skinless chicken breasts

CANDIED WALNUTS
Makes about 2 cups

1 pound walnut halves

1/4 cup honey

3 tablespoons brown sugar

CRANBERRY PURÉE

1/2 cup dried cranberries

1 tablespoon minced garlic

2 cups apple cider vinegar

1 cinnamon stick

1 cup packed brown sugar

TO PREPARE THE PURÉE, in a saucepan, combine the cranberries, garlic, vinegar, cinnamon stick, and brown sugar over medium-high heat. Simmer for 10 to 15 minutes, until reduced by half. Add the broth and simmer for 5 to 10 minutes. Remove the cinnamon stick and transfer the mixture to a blender. Purée until smooth; it should have a corn syrup–like consistency. Season with the salt and pepper.

TO PREPARE THE SALAD, place a large skillet over medium heat and add the oil. Add the carrots, green onions, and garlic and cook for 5 minutes. Add the quinoa and toss until well coated. Add the broth and cinnamon stick. Simmer, stirring occasionally, for 15 to 20 minutes, until the quinoa is tender and all the liquid has been absorbed. Season with salt and pepper. Remove from the heat and allow to cool completely.

Place a scoop of the quinoa in the center of each plate. Cut the chicken into 5 slices on the diagonal and arrange on the quinoa. Sprinkle the candied walnuts over the salad and drizzle the cranberry purée over the chicken. Serve at once.

1 cup chicken broth

1/4 teaspoon kosher salt

1/2 teaspoon freshly ground black pepper

SALAD

1/2 tablespoon vegetable oil

1/4 cup diced carrots

1/4 cup thinly sliced green onions

1/2 tablespoon minced garlic

1/2 pound quinoa

2 cups chicken broth

1/2 cinnamon stick

Kosher salt and freshly ground black pepper

"We have a policy at home: no kid dinners. We don't cater to our children's likes and dislikes. They have to at least try everything. Dinner is family time and everybody eats the same thing. I've also discovered that kids are more likely to eat a meal that they've helped prepare."

SEARED SCALLOPS with Celery Root Purée and Blood Orange Sauce

Serves 4

"I'm pretty much obsessed with seasonal fresh food," Tim says, "and this is an appetizer I came up with in the winter, when blood oranges are in season. Their flavor and color make a perfect match for the sweetness and subtlety of scallops." Here, a purée of celery root and potatoes rounds out the plate. "Basically, it's comfort food with a little twist. Everyone loves mashed potatoes. The celery root adds an appley sweetness that people really like—even if they can't exactly figure out what it is they're tasting."

TO PREPARE THE PURÉE, melt the butter in a saucepan over medium heat. Add the celery root and leek and cook for 3 to 5 minutes, until the leeks begin to soften and become fragrant but not brown. Add the potatoes and chicken broth, bring to a simmer, and cook until the celery root is very tender and the liquid is mostly reduced, 25 to 30 minutes. Drain well, reserving the liquid. Run the vegetables through a food mill or ricer to form a smooth purée. Add the cream, salt, and pepper, and reserved cooking liquid (it should look like a loose potato purée). Taste for seasoning and keep warm.

TO PREPARE THE SAUCE, combine the blood orange juice and ginger in a small saucepan over medium-high heat. Boil for 8 to 10 minutes, until reduced by half; you should have about $1/2$ cup. Remove from the heat and whisk in the butter. Season to taste with salt and pepper and keep warm.

Pat the scallops dry and season liberally on both sides with salt and pepper. Heat the oil in a large sauté pan over high heat until it shimmers. Add the scallops and sear for about $1^1/2$ minutes per side, until caramelized and golden brown.

To serve, place a dollop of the celery root purée in the center of 4 warmed plates. Place 2 seared scallops on top of each serving and drizzle the sauce around. Garnish with the minced chives and blood orange segments and serve at once.

CELERY ROOT PURÉE

2 tablespoons unsalted butter

2 celery root (celeriac), peeled and diced (about 4 cups)

1 cup thinly sliced leek, white and light green parts only

$1^1/2$ cups peeled and diced Yukon gold potatoes

3 cups chicken broth

$1/4$ cup heavy cream

$1/2$ teaspoon salt

$1/2$ teaspoon freshly ground black pepper

BLOOD ORANGE SAUCE

1 cup freshly squeezed blood orange juice (from 4 oranges), plus segments for garnish

$1/2$ teaspoon minced fresh ginger

2 tablespoons unsalted butter

Salt and freshly ground black pepper

8 diver sea scallops (about 12 ounces)

Salt and freshly ground black pepper

1 tablespoon olive oil

1 tablespoon minced fresh chives, for garnish

CHICKEN BREASTS with Tomato-Basil Sauce

Serves 4

Sometimes when Tim teaches cooking classes for families and children, his own kids will join him onstage, and this no-fail chicken dish is one they've demonstrated together. It's a satisfying weeknight entrée that comes together in just a few minutes—and it's a great way to master the technique of deglazing and making a quick pan sauce. Tim suggests serving it with garlic mashed potatoes and sautéed green beans.

Season the chicken breasts on both sides with salt and pepper. Dredge in the flour and shake off any excess.

Combine the oil and 1 tablespoon of the butter in a large sauté pan over medium-high heat. When the oil is hot, place the chicken in the pan and cook, turning once, for 4 to 5 minutes on each side, until golden brown and cooked through. Remove from the pan and keep warm.

Add the shallot and garlic to the hot pan. Sauté for 1 minute, then add the vinegar to deglaze the pan, using a wooden spoon to scrape up all the browned bits on the bottom. Add the chicken broth and tomatoes and cook for 1 to 2 minutes, until reduced by half. Remove the pan from the heat. Stirring constantly, add the basil, remaining 2 tablespoons butter, and salt and pepper to taste. Stir until the butter is incorporated into the sauce.

Place a chicken breast on each plate and pour the sauce over. Serve at once.

4 boneless skinless chicken breasts

Salt and freshly ground black pepper

$1/4$ cup all-purpose flour

1 tablespoon olive oil

3 tablespoons unsalted butter, at room temperature

1 shallot, minced

2 cloves garlic, minced

2 tablespoons balsamic vinegar

$3/4$ cup chicken broth

16 grape tomatoes, halved

$1/4$ cup fresh basil, thinly sliced

Nancy Silverton started her culinary life at eighteen as a vegetarian cook at her college dorm. Today, she's one of the world's most recognized bakers. Following her dorm gig, she trained at Le Cordon Bleu in London and Ecole Lenôtre in Paris, and was assistant pastry chef at Michael's in Santa Monica and head pastry chef at Wolfgang Puck's Spago. In 1989, she and her then-husband Mark Peel opened Campanile in Los Angeles. Nancy dove headlong into the task of developing European-style hearth-baked breads, doing exhaustive research to create her own starters and recipes. The result was La Brea Bakery, a storefront adjacent to the restaurant, which quickly grew into a major wholesale company, bringing artisan bread to restaurants and grocery stores all across America. Nancy has written six successful cookbooks on topics ranging from baking and desserts to sandwiches and family cooking.

TUSCAN CHICKEN POTPIES

Serves 4

Several times a year, Nancy heads for Italy to eat, cook, and enjoy la dolce vita *with friends. Her Tuscan-inspired take on chicken potpie incorporates some of her favorite Italian flavor-boosting ingredients: prosciutto, arugula, Parmesan, and cannellini beans. She bakes her individual pies in Italian cereal bowls, topping them with a rich Parmesan–crème fraîche crust, flecked with prosciutto and chives.*

Nancy's fresh take on Mrs. Hering's Potpie, page 65

TO PREPARE THE FILLING, combine 12 cloves of the garlic, the radicchio, beans, arugula, and chicken in a large bowl and toss well.

Melt the butter in a saucepan over low heat. Add the remaining 4 cloves garlic, the salt, and flour and whisk to combine. Cook, stirring constantly, for 2 to 3 minutes to make a roux. Remove from the heat and stir in the chicken broth, cheese, prosciutto, and pepper. Return to the stovetop over high heat and bring to a boil. Whisk constantly for 5 to 7 minutes, until slightly thickened. Pour over the chicken mixture and stir to combine. Divide the filling evenly among four 12-ounce oven-safe cereal bowls and set aside to cool.

Position a rack at the top of the oven and preheat to 400°F.

TO PREPARE THE DOUGH, combine the flour, baking powder, salt, and the 3/4 cup cheese in a food processor or an electric mixer fitted with the paddle attachment. Mix on low speed until incorporated. Add the cubed butter and pulse a few times or mix on low speed until the consistency of a fine meal.

FILLING

16 cloves garlic, thinly sliced

8 leaves radicchio, torn into 1 by 1-inch pieces

1 cup canned cannellini beans, drained

1 cup arugula

1/2 pound roasted chicken, skinned and shredded

13 tablespoons unsalted butter

1/2 teaspoon salt

6 tablespoons unbleached all-purpose flour

4 cups low-sodium chicken broth

1/2 cup freshly grated Parmigiano-Reggiano cheese

8 slices prosciutto, torn into bite-size pieces

4 teaspoons freshly cracked black pepper

Transfer to a large bowl, toss in the chives, and make a well in the center. Add the crème fraîche and, using one hand, mix in the dry ingredients until just combined. The mixture will be a bit dry and crumbly. Wash and dry your hands and dust them with flour. Turn the dough out onto a lightly floured work surface and gently knead a few times to gather it into a ball. Roll the dough out to $1/4$ inch thick and cut into four 5-inch rounds.

Press the pieces of prosciutto into the dough about $1/2$ inch apart. Place a round of dough on top of each bowl and brush with the melted butter. Sprinkle with the 2 tablespoons cheese and the pepper.

Bake for 15 to 18 minutes, until the crusts are nicely browned. Serve hot.

DOUGH

$2^3/4$ cups unbleached pastry or unbleached all-purpose flour

1 tablespoon plus 1 teaspoon baking powder

2 teaspoons kosher salt

$3/4$ cup plus 2 tablespoons freshly grated Parmigiano-Reggiano cheese

2 tablespoons unsalted butter, cut into $1/2$-inch cubes and frozen

$1/2$ cup minced fresh chives

1 cup crème fraîche or sour cream

1 to 2 prosciutto slices, torn into small pieces

7 tablespoons unsalted butter, melted

1 teaspoon freshly cracked black pepper

"My dad made me a little teak salt box with compartments for kosher salt, Maldon salt, and fleur de sel. I take it with me wherever I'm cooking. The thing about salt and pepper is to season every single layer, every step of the way, and taste as you go. That's how you build flavor.

OPEN-FACED ROASTED TURKEY SANDWICH
with Avocado, Watercress, Pickled Jalapeños, and Chipotle Mayonnaise

Serves 4

Nancy's got some serious sandwich credentials, from her Thursday Sandwich Nights at Campanile to the panini she's created for La Brea Bakery at Marshall Field's to Nancy Silverton's Sandwich Book. So, naturally, for her fresh take, she chose the most classic sandwich of all, the Field's Special. In her Latin-inspired version, the turkey's the same, but instead of bacon, lettuce, and Thousand Island, there's a smoky chipotle mayo, fresh watercress, pickled jalapeños, and big chunks of avocado. Maldon salt, an English sea salt, adds an extra hit of flavor and a delicate crunch.

Nancy's fresh take on Field's Special, page 40

TO PREPARE THE MAYONNAISE, whisk together the mayonnaise, oil, and lemon juice in a small bowl. Add the chiles, cilantro, half of the garlic, and salt to taste and stir to combine. Taste and adjust the seasoning with more garlic, salt, and lemon juice as needed.

To assemble the sandwiches, toast the bread on a grill press or in the oven and rub on one side with the garlic clove. Spread 1 tablespoon of the chipotle mayonnaise on each piece of bread. Pile the watercress on the bread, enough to cover. Drizzle with the oil, sprinkle with the salt, and add a couple drops of the lime juice. Rumple the turkey on top. Evenly divide the avocado on top of the turkey. Season the avocado with oil, salt, and lime juice. Arrange the jalapeños and cilantro leaves on top of the sandwiches and serve at once.

CHIPOTLE MAYONNAISE

1 cup mayonnaise

2 tablespoons extra virgin olive oil

2 tablespoons freshly squeezed lemon juice, plus more to taste

1 1/2 teaspoons puréed canned chipotle chiles in adobo

1/4 cup finely chopped cilantro leaves

4 large cloves garlic, grated or minced

Salt

4 slices La Brea Bakery Country White Sourdough bread

1 clove garlic, halved

1 bunch Live Gourmet watercress or other watercress, stems removed

Extra virgin olive oil

Maldon salt

Juice of 1/2 lime

1 1/2 pounds turkey breast, thinly sliced

2 ripe avocados, sliced lengthwise

2 pickled jalapeños (or more, to taste), seeded and thinly sliced lengthwise

1/4 cup whole cilantro leaves

"I like food to look natural on the plate, like it just kind of fell from the sky—but in a beautiful way. Light and airy, not patted down. With sandwiches, I go for the layered look, and fluff up every layer as I go."

CELERY AND HERB SALAD
with Stracciatella Cheese and Celery Leaf Pesto

Serves 4

"Some salads are light and fresh, others are bold and surprising," says Nancy. "Somehow, this one is all those things at the same time!" It's a tangle of whole fresh herbs and crunchy celery tossed in a lemony vinaigrette, topped with soft Stracciatella cheese and a zippy celery leaf pesto. "Stracciatella is a proprietary cheese made by a Los Angeles mozzarella company," she notes. "It's the stringlike curds from the inside of a burrata cheese. If you can't track it down, a soft ricotta cheese will work nicely. If your ricotta isn't soft, add a little extra virgin olive oil to soften it."

TO PREPARE THE PESTO, preheat the oven to 325°F. Spread the pine nuts on a baking sheet and toast for 8 to 10 minutes, until lightly browned. Increase the oven temperature to 350°F. Using a mortar and pestle, pulverize the pine nuts, garlic, parsley, celery leaves, and salt into a smooth paste. (Or finely chop the ingredients and smash with a knife to purée.) Slowly drizzle in the olive oil and add the cheese, mixing well to incorporate. Just before serving, add the lemon juice and lemon zest, and season to taste with salt.

TO PREPARE THE CROUTONS, adjust the oven rack to the middle position. Place the bread pieces on a baking sheet and drizzle with the oil. Place in the oven and toast until golden brown.

TO PREPARE THE VINAIGRETTE, in a small bowl, whisk together the lemon juice, olive oil, and shallot. Season with the salt and pepper to taste.

To assemble the salad, combine the chervil, tarragon, parsley, chives, basil, celery, green onions, and croutons in a large bowl. Season with the Maldon salt and toss well. Add a conservative amount of the vinaigrette to the salad, just enough to moisten, and save the remaining dressing for drizzling around the plate.

CELERY LEAF PESTO

1/8 cup pine nuts

1/2 large clove garlic

1/2 bunch fresh flat-leaf parsley

1/4 cup tender celery leaves

1/8 teaspoon kosher salt

1/2 cup extra virgin olive oil

1/8 to 1/4 cup freshly grated Parmigiano-Reggiano cheese

Juice of 1/2 lemon

Zest of 1/2 lemon

CROUTONS

1 sourdough baguette, sliced into 1 1/2 to 2-inch pieces

1/2 cup extra virgin olive oil

VINAIGRETTE

6 tablespoons freshly squeezed lemon juice (about 3 lemons)

6 tablespoons extra virgin olive oil

1 shallot, finely chopped

1 teaspoon kosher salt

Freshly cracked black pepper

1/2 cup whole fresh chervil leaves

Divide the greens among 4 plates (preferably use oversized soup plates with a wide rim), mounding them in the center. Drizzle the extra dressing on the plate around the greens. Make an indentation in the middle of the greens and spoon on 2 ounces of the Stracciatella cheese. Season with a little more Maldon salt. Spoon 1 tablespoon of the celery leaf pesto onto each serving and serve the rest on the side.

1/2 cup whole fresh tarragon leaves

1/2 cup whole fresh flat-leaf parsley leaves

1/2 cup snipped fresh chives

1/2 cup whole tiny fresh basil leaves

1/8 cup peeled and diagonally sliced celery

1/8 cup diagonally sliced green onions

Maldon salt or sea salt

8 ounces Stracciatella cheese

NANCY'S BURGERS

Serves 6 | *A huge party centered around an outdoor fireplace is Nancy's favorite way to entertain, and that often means burgers, especially when her kids are involved. Here's her idea of hamburger heaven, buffet-style—a choice of three mayos (including "the good old store-bought kind—you've got to have it"), three kinds of cheese, bacon, avocado, heirloom tomatoes, and some nice seeded buns. For the ground beef, she recommends asking your butcher for her custom blend: $2^3/_4$ pounds of whole prime chuck (10 to 15 percent fat) ground with 4 to 6 ounces of prime sirloin (13 percent fat).*

TO PREPARE THE GARLIC MAYONNAISE, whisk together the mayonnaise, oil, and lemon juice in a small bowl. Stir in the salt and half of the garlic. Taste and adjust the seasoning with more garlic, salt, and lemon juice as needed.

TO PREPARE THE ANCHOVY AND OLIVE MAYONNAISE, measure out $1/_2$ cup of the garlic mayonnaise into a separate small bowl. Add the anchovy paste, tapenade, and parsley. Stir to mix.

Place a skillet over medium heat and fry the bacon for about 8 minutes, until just short of crispiness to avoid shattering when eating. Transfer to paper towels to drain.

Cut the avocados into quarters and place in a serving dish. Sprinkle lightly with the lemon juice, add the chives, and toss. Season to taste with salt and pepper.

Arrange the tomato slices on a plate and season lightly with salt and pepper. Arrange the onion slices on a plate and season lightly with sea salt and pepper.

Crumble the blue cheese and cheddar into separate bowls. Slice the Gruyère with a cheese plane onto a serving plate.

GARLIC MAYONNAISE

1 cup mayonnaise

2 tablespoons extra virgin olive oil

1 tablespoon plus 1 teaspoon freshly squeezed lemon juice, plus more to taste

$1/_4$ teaspoon kosher salt, plus more to taste

4 large cloves garlic, grated or minced (about 1 heaping tablespoon)

ANCHOVY AND OLIVE MAYONNAISE

$1/_2$ cup Garlic Mayonnaise

$1/_2$ teaspoon anchovy paste, or 3 anchovy fillets in oil, smashed with the back of a knife

2 teaspoons olive tapenade

2 teaspoons finely chopped fresh flat-leaf parsley

12 strips applewood-smoked bacon

2 ripe avocados

1 teaspoon freshly squeezed lemon juice

2 tablespoons snipped fresh chives

Preheat a gas grill to high, prepare a fire in a charcoal grill, or place a seasoned cast-iron skillet over high heat. Being careful not to overwork the meat, shape the ground beef into 6 patties, about 2 inches thick and 4 inches in diameter. Sprinkle both sides of the patties with about $1/2$ teaspoon of kosher salt and 4 to 6 grindings of black pepper. Place the burgers on the grill rack or in the skillet. Sear them until they can be turned without sticking, then turn them. For rare, cook about 4 minutes, then flip and cook another 4 minutes (for medium-rare, 5 minutes on each side; for medium, 6 minutes).

As the burgers are cooking, brush the cut sides of the buns with oil. Place the buns, cut side down, on the grill rack or in the pan, for 1 to 2 minutes, to toast. Just before the burgers are done cooking, sprinkle with a little good-quality sea salt, then top with one of the cheeses and let it melt.

To serve, have guests place lettuce, onion, tomato, bacon, and avocado on the bottom half of their toasted bun. Place the burger on top, then the top of the bun. Serve the burgers with the Garlic Mayonnaise, Anchovy and Olive mayonnaise, regular mayonnaise, ketchup, mustard, pepper-oncini, and pickles.

Sea salt and freshly ground black pepper

1 large ripe heirloom, Brandywine, Russian, or Beefsteak tomato, sliced $1/4$ inch thick

$1/2$ red onion, thinly sliced

3 ounces blue cheese

3 ounces cheddar cheese

3 ounces Gruyère cheese

3 pounds ground beef

3 teaspoons kosher salt

6 large sesame or poppy seed hamburger buns

Extra virgin olive oil

6 (5-inch-wide) iceberg lettuce leaf halves

Heinz Ketchup

Best Foods Mayonnaise

Dijon mustard, smooth and coarse-grained

Tuscan pepperoncini (such as Mezzetta brand)

Dill pickles, sliced lengthwise into quarters or eighths

Ming Tsai is one of America's most popular East-West chefs. He started cooking as a teenager at his family's Chinese restaurant in Dayton, Ohio, then got a degree in mechanical engineering from Yale. But cooking kept calling his name, and he soon found himself in Paris, where he studied at Le Cordon Bleu and worked at two celebrated restaurants. After earning a master's in hotel administration at Cornell, he cooked for several high-profile restaurants around the country, developing a keen instinct for marrying Asian and Western flavors. That's what he brought to the table when he and his wife, Polly, opened Blue Ginger, a high-style East-West bistro in the Boston suburb of Wellesley. The restaurant received three stars from the *Boston Globe* in its first year and has been the "second most popular Boston Restaurant" in *Zagat* for the last three years. The author of two cookbooks, Ming hosted two Food Network series, *East Meets West: Cooking with Ming Tsai,* for which he won an Emmy award, and *Ming's Quest.* He is now the host of *Simply Ming* on public television.

SHRIMP AND ROOT VEGETABLE POTPIE with a Panko Crust

Serves 4

What does East-West comfort food look like? How about succulent shrimp and tender root vegetables in a sweet-spicy–carrot-chipotle sauce? Ming's light, easy topping of seasoned panko breadcrumbs adds just the right balance to those big flavors (and it's a great way to go if you're not one for rolling out pie dough).

Ming's fresh take on Mrs. Hering's Potpie, page 65

TO PREPARE THE SYRUP, bring the carrot juice to a gentle simmer in a large, nonreactive saucepan over low heat. Simmer for about 45 minutes, until all the liquid is evaporated, leaving a wet residue. With a heat-resistant rubber spatula, scrape the carrot juice residue from the pan and transfer to a blender. Add the chile and blend on high speed until smooth. With the motor running, add the oil in a slow, steady stream until the mixture is emulsified, then add the oil more quickly to prevent the sauce from breaking. Season to taste with salt and pepper. (The syrup will last for 2 weeks, refrigerated.)

TO PREPARE THE BREADCRUMBS, combine all of the ingredients in a bowl and mix well. (You can also use plain panko, without adding the spices.)

Preheat the oven to 375°F. To prepare the filling, heat a large stockpot over high heat. Add the oil and swirl to coat the pot. Add the onion and sauté, stirring, for about 2 minutes, until soft. Add the carrots, celery, sweet potato, and celery root and season with salt and pepper. Sauté for 4 minutes, until the vegetables begin to soften. Add the broth and simmer for about 15 minutes, until the liquid is reduced by half. Taste and adjust the seasoning as necessary. In a small bowl, whisk together the cornstarch and water. Add the cornstarch mixture to the pot and simmer for about 3 minutes, until lightly thickened. Add 1/4 cup of the carrot-chipotle syrup and mix well. Remove from the heat and allow to cool.

CARROT-CHIPOTLE SYRUP
Makes 4 cups

2 quarts fresh carrot juice

1 teaspoon chopped chipotle chile in adobo sauce

3/4 cup grapeseed oil

Kosher salt and cracked black pepper

SPICED PANKO BREADCRUMBS
Makes 4 cups

4 cups Japanese breadcrumbs (panko)

2 tablespoons dried thyme

2 tablespoons dried basil

1 tablespoon ground ginger

1 tablespoon coarsely ground black pepper

1 tablespoon ancho chile powder or regular chile powder

1 tablespoon kosher salt

FILLING

2 tablespoons grapeseed or canola oil

1 large onion, cut into 1/2-inch dice

8 ounces peeled baby carrots

4 celery stalks, cut into 1-inch pieces

1 large sweet potato, peeled and cut into 1/2-inch dice

Fold the shrimp into the cooled filling and divide among four 6- to 8-ounce ramekins. Divide 1¹/₂ cups of the spiced panko among the ramekins as topping (the remaining panko can be stored in the refrigerator for up to 3 weeks). Transfer the ramekins to a baking sheet and bake for about 20 minutes, until the filling is bubbling hot and the topping is browned. Drizzle the potpies with another ¹/₄ cup of the carrot-chipotle syrup and serve hot. (Any leftover syrup can be stored in the refrigerator for up to 2 weeks.)

1 large celery root or 1 additional sweet potato, peeled and cut into ¹/₂-inch dice

Kosher salt and cracked black pepper

2 cups vegetable or chicken broth

1 tablespoon cornstarch

1 tablespoon water

1¹/₂ pounds small shrimp, peeled and cleaned

TEA-SMOKED SALMON CARPACCIO with Jicama-Avocado Salad

Serves 4

"I try to maintain a healthy lifestyle and eat in a balanced way," says Ming, "and that means lots of lean protein. Salmon's a great choice—full of omega-3 fatty acids and vitamin E, which is a powerful antioxidant." This presentation is health and harmony on a plate—an easy first course or light entrée with "tons of flavor and all the elegance of a classic beef carpaccio."

TO PREPARE THE VINAIGRETTE, in a blender, combine the mustard, shallots, lemon juice, and lime juice; blend until smooth. With the blender running, slowly drizzle in the olive oil. Check for flavor and season with salt and pepper.

In a bowl, combine the jicama, avocado, and ¹/₂ cup of the vinaigrette; toss gently to avoid bruising the avocado. To serve, lay 3 slices of the smoked salmon on each plate, top with the jicama-avocado salad, and garnish with the remaining vinaigrette. Serve at once.

VINAIGRETTE

2 tablespoons Dijon mustard

3 shallots, roughly chopped

Juice of 2 lemons

Juice of 2 limes

1 cup extra virgin olive oil

Kosher salt and freshly ground black pepper

1 jicama, julienned

1 avocado, cut into ¹/₄-inch dice

12 slices Perona Farms Five-Spice Chile Tea Rubbed Smoked Salmon

MOM'S 3-2-1 SHRIMP

Serves 4

"Three vinegar, two sugar, one soy." That's the basic formula for Ming's mom's all-purpose sauce and marinade. "It's good with all kinds of stuff," says Ming. "I've even tossed crispy chicken livers in it, Buffalo wing–style." Here, he uses the sauce in a quick sauté of shrimp, tomatoes, and edamame. He recommends serving the dish over creamy mashed potatoes.

Ming's fresh take on New Orleans–Style Barbecued Shrimp, page 53

TO PREPARE THE SAUCE, place a saucepan lightly coated with oil over high heat. Add the garlic and ginger and sauté until softened, about 2 minutes. In a bowl, whisk together the rice vinegar, sugar, and soy sauce until the sugar dissolves. Deglaze the saucepan with this mixture, bring to a simmer, and cook until reduced by half. Season with salt and pepper. Transfer the sauce to a blender and add the butter, a few cubes at a time, blending on high speed until smooth. Check the flavor and correct the seasoning as necessary.

Place a saucepan or wok lightly coated with oil over high heat. Add the white part of the green onions and sauté until softened, about 2 minutes. Add the shrimp, season with salt and pepper, and sauté until just pink, 2 to 3 minutes. Add the tomatoes, edamame, and ¹/₂ cup of the sauce and mix well. Taste and adjust the seasoning as necessary. Transfer to a serving platter, garnish with the green part of the green onions, and serve family style.

3-2-1 SAUCE

2 tablespoons minced garlic

1 tablespoon minced fresh ginger

1 ¹/₂ cups naturally brewed rice vinegar

1 cup sugar

¹/₂ cup naturally brewed soy sauce

Kosher salt and freshly ground black pepper

¹/₂ cup cold unsalted butter, cut into ¹/₂-inch cubes

4 green onions, thinly sliced on the diagonal, whites and greens separated

1 pound large shrimp, peeled and deveined

Kosher salt and freshly ground black pepper

1 cup ¹/₂-inch-diced tomatoes

1 cup shelled edamame

Grapeseed or canola oil, for cooking

"My kids aren't picky eaters. They're more like connoisseurs. The other day, one of my sons tasted something I made and said, 'Daddy, is there enough salt in here?' I said, 'I'm a chef. Just eat it.' Then I tasted it. Of course, he was right."

RED ROAST DUCK LEGS

"The aroma of red roast is a favorite memory from my childhood," says Ming, who recalls how his grandfather and father would cook up batch after batch of red roast whole ducks and pork shoulders. "There's nothing better than the fragrance of soy, rock candy, star anise, and ginger simmering on the stove," he says. "It reminds me of holidays spent with family, surrounded by great food." Rock sugar, sold in amber-colored chunks in Chinese or Southeast Asian markets, is worth tracking down. It imparts a rich flavor and a beautiful sheen to the glaze.

In a nonreactive stockpot, combine the wines, soy sauces, and water. Bring to a boil over high heat and add the duck legs. If the liquid doesn't cover the duck, add more water. Bring to a boil again, then decrease the heat and simmer, periodically skimming off the scum, for about 30 minutes.

Add the rock sugar, ginger, garlic, white part of the green onions, star anise, chiles, cinnamon sticks, and orange and stir to dissolve the sugar. Simmer until the duck is very tender and just falling off the bone, $1^1/_2$ to 2 hours. During the last 10 minutes of cooking, add the bok choy. Using a slotted spoon, transfer the duck and bok choy to a plate and cover with aluminum foil.

Strain and skim the stock and return it to the pot. Place over high heat and reduce until lightly syrupy, about 20 minutes. Transfer the duck legs to a serving platter and surround with the bok choy. Glaze the duck with the sauce, garnish with the green part of the green onions, and serve.

1 (750-ml) bottle dry red wine

2 cups Shaoxing wine, or 1 cup dry sherry

1 cup dark soy sauce

3 cups soy sauce

4 cups water

12 duck legs

2 pounds rock sugar or dark brown sugar

1 (5-inch) piece fresh ginger, cut into long $^1/_4$-inch slices

1 head garlic, unpeeled and halved horizontally

2 bunches green onions, white part sliced into 3-inch lengths, green part sliced $^1/_8$ inch thick

2 star anise

3 dried Thai bird chiles

2 cinnamon sticks

1 orange, washed and halved

8 baby bok choy, halved and cored

Takashi Yagihashi got his first taste of professional cooking as a teenager in his hometown of Mito, Japan, where he studied with the chef of a local restaurant. In 1981, the restaurant's owner decided to expand to the United States and asked Takashi to help. He spent the next several years in Chicago, mastering the techniques of French cooking and nouvelle cuisine at several of the city's leading restaurants, including Les Plumes, Yoshi's Café, and Ambria. In 1996, he was invited to open the spectacular Tribute in Farmington Hills, Michigan, which the *New York Times* called "perhaps the finest restaurant between New York and Chicago." He is now the executive chef of Okada at the Wynn Las Vegas hotel, where he has created a menu of contemporary Japanese food influenced by his French and American training.

KUROBUTA SHORT RIB POTPIE

Serves 4

Takashi's "deconstructed" potpie features slowly simmered short ribs topped with vegetables, potatoes, and tofu, with crispy wontons standing in for the crust. He likes to use Kurobuta pork, which is cut from Berkshire black hogs and is more marbled than most commercial pork, making it extra moist and flavorful.

Takashi's fresh take on Mrs. Hering's Potpie, page 65

TO PREPARE THE BROTH, place a stockpot over high heat and add the oil. When the oil is hot, add the pork and sear until browned on all sides. Add the water, carrot, onion, celery, garlic, ginger, bay leaves, leek, star anise, and cinnamon and bring to a boil. Decrease the heat to medium-low and braise for about 3 hours, until the meat is fork-tender. Pass the broth through a fine-mesh strainer, discarding the vegetables and reserving the meat and the broth.

TO PREPARE THE DASHI, wipe the kelp with a wet towel. Place the kelp in a pot and cover with the water. Let stand for 30 to 60 minutes to draw flavor from the kelp. Place the pot over medium heat. When the water is almost boiling, remove and discard the kelp. Bring the water to a boil, then add the bonito flakes all at once. When the water returns to a boil, remove the pot from the heat. Let steep for 5 minutes. Strain the dashi through a double thickness of cheesecloth and discard the bonito flakes.

TO PREPARE THE FILLING, in a large pot over medium-high heat, combine 1 quart of the pork broth, short ribs, dashi, sake, and mirin and bring to a boil. Add the sugar and stir until dissolved, then add $1/3$ cup of the soy sauce. Decrease the heat to low to achieve a simmer, then gradually add the remaining $1/3$ cup soy sauce. Simmer for about 1 hour, until slightly thickened

BROTH

$1/4$ cup grapeseed oil

12 (3-ounce) boneless pork short ribs

2 quarts water

1 carrot, chopped

1 onion, chopped

1 celery stalk, chopped

4 cloves garlic

1 (1-inch) piece fresh ginger, sliced

2 bay leaves

1 leek, white part only, chopped

2 to 3 pieces star anise

1 stick cinnamon

DASHI

5 cups dried kelp

$4^{1}/_{2}$ cups cold water

2 cups bonito flakes

Prepare the garnish vegetables about 20 minutes before serving the dish. Bring a saucepan full of water to a simmer. Add the onions, carrot, sassafras, daikon, and potatoes and simmer for 20 minutes, until soft. Remove from the water with a skimmer. Add the tofu and pea pods and cook for about 1 minute. Immediately drain and cool under running water.

Pour the oil into a large skillet to a depth of 2 inches and place over medium heat. When the oil has reached 275°F, add the wonton skins and fry for 3 to 4 minutes, until golden brown and crispy. Transfer to paper towels to drain.

Divide the garnish vegetables among 4 large, deep bowls. Add 3 short ribs to each serving, then pour in some of the broth to cover the vegetables. Top each serving with some cilantro leaves, green onion, and ginger. Lay 2 wonton skins on top of each bowl. Top with a pinch of the shichimi-togarashi and serve at once.

FILLING

1 1/4 cups sake

1 1/4 cups mirin (sweet sake)

1/2 cup sugar

2/3 cup soy sauce

GARNISH VEGETABLES

12 pearl onions

12 oblique slices carrot

12 oblique slices fresh sassafras

12 (1 1/2-inch) daikon cubes

8 small fingerling potatoes, peeled

12 (1 1/2-inch) firm tofu cubes

12 fresh pea pods

Peanut or vegetable oil, for deep frying

8 (4 by 4-inch) wonton skins

1/4 cup cilantro leaves

1/4 cup julienned green onions

1/4 cup julienned fresh ginger

4 pinches shichimi-togarashi (Japanese dried mixed chile powder)

"I spent sixteen years in Chicago and nine in Detroit. When the seasons change there—woof!—watch out. But Japanese cooking is great for extreme weather. In the winter, you can do braising and slow-roasting, and in the summer you have beautiful, light salads and raw fish. I like to feel the seasons changing—and then I change my cooking to match."

SEARED TUNA SALAD

with Baby Frisée, Mâche, and Endive and Sweet Onion–Yuzu Dressing

Serves 4 | *Not your average tuna salad, Takashi's starts with thin slices of* tataki—*tuna loin (bonito and hamachi are particularly good) that's quickly seared on the outside, then chilled, sliced, and dressed with* ponzu, *a Japanese citrus vinaigrette. The tuna is served alongside a salad of tender greens. "Mâche, baby frisée, endive," says Takashi, smiling. "I love those guys."*

Takashi's fresh take on Twisted Tuna Salad, page 78

Slice the tuna into twenty 2¹/₂-inch-wide, 1-inch-long, and ¹/₈-inch-thick slices. Place a nonstick sauté over high heat and add the oil. A few at a time, add the tuna pieces and sear quickly for just 5 seconds on each side. Transfer to the refrigerator until ready to serve.

TO PREPARE THE GARLIC CHIPS, heat the oil in a small saucepan over medium-high heat until it reaches 300°F. Add the garlic and cook for 5 to 6 minutes, until golden brown. Transfer to paper towels to drain and sprinkle lightly with salt.

TO PREPARE THE DRESSING, combine all the ingredients in a bowl and whisk well. The dressing can be refrigerated for up to 1 week.

Toss the mâche, frisée, endive, and radish together in a bowl. To serve, place about 1 cup of the mixed greens on the left side of a large rectangular plate. Lay 5 slices of the tuna side by side to the right of the greens. Scatter the ginger and chives over the tuna and top each slice with 1 garlic chip. Finish by drizzling 2 tablespoons of the dressing on the greens and tuna slices. Serve chilled.

8 ounces sashimi-quality tuna loin

1 teaspoon olive oil

GARLIC CHIPS

2 cups olive oil

¹/₄ cup very thinly sliced garlic

Salt

DRESSING

¹/₄ cup yuzu juice, or 2 tablespoons each freshly squeezed lemon and lime juice

1 tablespoon grapeseed oil

2 tablespoons grated onion

1 teaspoon very finely grated ginger

¹/₂ teaspoon very finely grated garlic

3 tablespoons soy sauce

¹/₄ cup sugar

1 drop sesame oil

Freshly ground black pepper

1 cup mâche

1 cup baby frisée

1 cup endive, cut into 1-inch lengths

¹/₂ cup sliced pink radish (¹/₈ inch thick)

¹/₈ cup julienned fresh ginger

¹/₈ cup chives, cut into 2-inch lengths

SUKIYAKI BOWL

Serves 4

"Sukiyaki-don, a rustic, home-style dish, is my son and daughter's favorite," says Takashi. "We make it all the time at home because it's quick and comforting." One secret for success is to use the best beef your budget will allow. Kobe beef is ideal, but it's expensive and hard to find, so Takashi recommends asking your butcher to slice rib-eye on a meat slicer. Shirataki are clear, gelatinous noodles made from an Asian root vegetable. Look for them in the refrigerated section of Japanese markets.

TO PREPARE THE SAUCE, combine the ingredients in a small bowl and stir until the sugar is dissolved.

Bring a small saucepan of water to a boil and add the shirataki. Parboil for 5 minutes to remove the limestone odor. Drain well.

Arrange the sliced onion, cabbage, mushrooms, green onions, spinach, tofu, and shirataki in an even layer in a 10-inch skillet. Add 2 cups of the sukiyaki sauce. Cook over high heat until it starts to come to a boil, then arrange the sliced meat on top. Decrease the heat to medium and pour the eggs over the top. Cover the pan and simmer for about 90 seconds, until the eggs are evenly cooked. Make sure there is adequate liquid left in the skillet. If not, add 1 more cup of the sukiyaki sauce.

Place about 1¹/₂ cups of the rice in each bowl. Divide the sukiyaki equally among the bowls. Spoon 1 tablespoon of the cooking broth over each and serve at once.

JAPANESE-STYLE RICE: An electric rice cooker is ideal for making perfect Japanese-style rice, which will cling together and have a delicate, soft texture. For every cup of medium-grain white rice, use 2¹/₄ to 2¹/₂ cups of water. A cup of raw rice cooked this way will yield about 2¹/₂ cups of cooked rice.

SUKIYAKI SAUCE

1 cup mirin

1 cup soy sauce

1 cup sake

1 tablespoon sugar

1 cup shirataki noodles

1 small onion, sliced

3 cups napa cabbage, sliced into 2-inch ribbons

1 (3¹/₂-ounce) package enoki mushrooms, stumps trimmed off

2 bunches green onions, cut into 2-inch lengths

¹/₂ bunch fresh spinach, cut into 2-inch ribbons

¹/₂ block firm tofu, cubed

14 ounces beef rib-eye roast, very thinly sliced

4 eggs, lightly beaten

6 cups steamed white rice

SALAD OF OCTOPUS with Hearts of Palm, Cucumber, and Seaweed

Serves 6

This is a classic Japanese sunomono *salad of cucumber, seaweed, and seafood in a light citrus dressing. Takashi especially likes it with octopus. "If you don't think cooking an octopus sounds like fun, you can find it already cooked in most Japanese fish markets," he says. And if even precooked octopus is not your thing, you can use squid, shrimp, lobster, snapper, or hamachi. Usukuchi soy sauce, sold at Japanese food markets, is lighter, thinner, and saltier than regular soy sauce.*

TO PREPARE THE VINAIGRETTE, combine all the ingredients in a saucepan over medium-high heat and mix well. Bring to a boil, then remove from the heat and refrigerate until chilled.

In the middle of each of 6 shallow soup bowls, place some of the cucumber and seaweed side by side. Add the oba leaves next to the seaweed. If using fresh hearts of palm, place the slices on top of the cucumber and seaweed. If using canned hearts of palm, place 2 slices lengthwise on top of the seaweed and cucumber. Top with the sliced octopus. Place the shiso leaves on the octopus and sprinkle with the sesame seeds. Arrange the tomatoes around the bowls, and drizzle about 2 tablespoons of the vinaigrette over each serving. Serve immediately.

"Fresh seafood should smell like a soft ocean breeze.
I grew up by the seashore, so that smell always
makes me happy."

CITRUS VINAIGRETTE

Juice of 2 lemons

Juice of 2 limes

1/2 cup rice vinegar

1 tablespoon plus 1 teaspoon sugar

1/2 teaspoon salt

Pinch of crushed red pepper flakes

1 teaspoon usukuchi soy sauce

1/4 cup water or dashi

6 ounces Japanese or seedless English cucumber, very thinly sliced (about 1 cup)

6 ounces fresh or reconstituted dried seaweed (dried seaweed should be soaked in water for 10 minutes, then drained)

6 oba leaves

9 ounces fresh hearts of palm sliced paper-thin and rinsed, or 6 canned hearts of palm, halved

12 ounces fresh cooked octopus, sliced 1/8 inch thick

6 micro red shiso leaves (optional)

1 teaspoon black sesame seeds

6 yellow teardrop tomatoes, halved

6 red teardrop tomatoes, halved

INDEX

ACKNOWLEDGMENTS

We would like to thank Warren Wolfe, vice president of food services at Marshall Field's, the idea man behind this book, for his rare combination of vision, clarity, enthusiasm, and good humor. Thanks also to Marshall Field's President Frank Guzzetta for writing the foreword and for his excitement about this project from the outset.

It's a joy to work with the Marshall Field's team and to be constantly surprised and delighted by their refreshingly positive energy and graciousness. Corporate Executive Chefs Tim Scott and Elizabeth Brown developed, adapted, tested, and oversaw the photography of the recipes with skill, finesse, and a generous helping of goodwill, ably assisted by Susan Johnson. Debbie Thompson coordinated and tracked the many moving parts of this project, never missing a beat, and chefs Chris Morse and Jason Henson-Myers provided invaluable assistance with the food photography at the Walnut Room. Special thanks to Kelly Lainsbury for her unwavering dedication to getting it right, and to Amy Meadows, Marisa Reeves, Aurora Kessler, Tasha Ziemer, Michelle Barron, Heidi Zimmerman, and the staff of the Marshall Field's archives for reviewing the manuscript and providing historical information and photography. We are also particularly grateful to Mark Krisco, who curated an exhibit on the culinary history of food at Marshall Field's on which parts of the introduction to this book were based.

We thank the Field's Culinary Council—Rick Bayless, Elizabeth Brown, Tom Douglas, Todd English, Tyler Florence, Gale Gand, Andrea Robinson, Marcus Samuelsson, Tim Scott, Nancy Silverton, Ming Tsai, and Takashi Yagihashi—for contributing their recipes and ideas, and for making time for our photo session in Napa.

We are grateful to Karl Benson, managing partner of Cooks of Crocus Hill, who steered us to Marshall Field's and helped define the book's style and direction, and to Dennis Hayes and Lorena Jones of Ten Speed Press, for referring us to Karl and for their ongoing support.

Maren Caruso, a true artist and gracious collaborator, shot hundreds of spectacular photos on location and in her studio, giving us a dazzling range of options to choose from. We thank her and her team—assistants Faiza Ali and Hans Kwiotek, and retouchers Mark Rutherford and Lauren Burke—for their talent and their "sure, we can do that!" attitude. Stylist George Dolese never fails to bring beauty, focus, and grace to his work, and we're grateful to him and associate food stylist Elisabet der Nederlanden for making the food in this book look as wonderful as it tastes. Thanks also to stylist Kim Konecny for her great work on the cover shot. Thank you Susie Heller for opening your home to us for our Culinary Council shoot, and Amy Vogler for prepping, schlepping, and organizing that shoot with such good-natured professionalism.

We thank our editor Holly Taines White for her thoroughness and attention to detail, Meghan Keeffe for editorial support and eagle-eyed proofreading, Hal Belmont of Overseas Printing, and indexer Ken DellaPenta.

Many thanks to the Minnesota Historical Society for providing information on Dayton's and Michael Hauser, author of *Hudson's: Detroit's Legendary Department Store,* for helping with Hudson's research.

We would like to express our gratitude to the Marshall Field's guests and team members who agreed to appear in photographs throughout this book: Kathleen Normile (page ii), Devon Everage (page 5), Estelle Jones Langston (page 14), Elyse Knoll (page 88), Mr. and Mrs. Joseph Clark (page106), and Erica Becker (pages 107 and 111).

And finally, we thank the team members of Marshall Field's and the loyal family of Field's guests. Together, you have created a part of American culinary history, and we hope this book makes you proud and brings you joy.

Catherine Jacobes and Steve Siegelman
Book Kitchen

BOOK KITCHEN
www.bookkitchen.com

Text: **Steve Siegelman**

Design: **Catherine Jacobes**

Photography: **Maren Caruso**

Photography assistance: **Faiza Ali** and **Hans Kwiotek**

Food stylist: **George Dolese**

Assistant food stylist: **Elisabet der Nederlanden**

Food stylist for front cover image: **Kim Konecny**

Digital imaging and prepress: **Mark Rutherford**

Copyeditor: **Holly Taines White**

Proofreader: **Meghan Keeffe**

Indexer: **Ken DellaPenta**

Library of Congress Cataloging-in-Publication Data is available.

ISBN 0-9779890-0-3

First printing, 2006

Printed and bound in China by Overseas Printing Corporation

2 3 4 5 6 7 8 9 10 — 10 09 08 07 06